The Metapsychol
Christopher Bolla

CW00495484

The Metapsychology of Christopher Bollas: An Introduction explores Bollas's extraordinarily wide contribution to contemporary psychoanalysis. The book aims to introduce and explain the fundamentals of Bollas's theory of the mind in a systematic way, addressing many of the questions that commonly arise when people approach his work.

Through chapters on topics such as the receptive unconscious, idiom, the unthought known, and the implications of Bollas's metapsychology for the technique of free association, the book enables the reader to acquire an understanding of his unique psychoanalytic language, to grasp the conceptual building blocks of his thinking and how these interrelate, and to appreciate the theoretical and clinical coherence of his thinking.

The Metapsychology of Christopher Bollas: An Introduction will be of use to psychoanalysts, psychotherapists and counsellors, as well as psychiatrists, psychologists and social workers wishing to explore the applications of psychoanalytic thinking to their practice. It will be of great value to trainees in these disciplines, as well as to postgraduate students and academics interested in contemporary psychoanalysis.

Sarah Nettleton is a psychoanalyst in London. Originally a piano accompanist, she has written on music and the internal world and on the psychodynamics of musical giftedness. For the past 7 years she has taught seminars on the work of Christopher Bollas extensively in the UK, and in Norway, Israel, France, the USA and Turkey.

The Metapsychology of Christopher Bollas

An Introduction

Sarah Nettleton

Routledge
Taylor & Francis Group

LONDON AND NEW YORK

First published 2017
by Routledge
2 Park Square, Milton Park, Abingdon, Oxon OX14 4RN

and by Routledge
711 Third Avenue, New York, NY 10017

Routledge is an imprint of the Taylor & Francis Group, an informa business

© 2017 Sarah Nettleton

British Library Cataloguing in Publication Data
A catalogue record for this book is available from the British Library

Library of Congress Cataloging-in-Publication Data
Names: Nettleton, Sarah, 1955– author.
Title: The metapsychology of Christopher Bollas : an introduction /
    Sarah Nettleton.
Description: Abingdon, Oxon ; New York, NY : Routledge, 2016. |
    Includes index.
Identifiers: LCCN 2015048761 | ISBN 9781138795549 (hardback) |
    ISBN 9781138795556 (pbk.) | ISBN 9781315758374 (ebook)
Subjects: LCSH: Bollas, Christopher. | Psychoanalysis. | Spiritualism.
Classification: LCC BF109.B6435 N47 2016 | DDC 150.19/5—dc23
LC record available at http://lccn.loc.gov/2015048761

ISBN: 978-1-138-79554-9 (hbk)
ISBN: 978-1-138-79555-6 (pbk)
ISBN: 978-1-315-75837-4 (ebk)

Typeset in Times New Roman
by Apex CoVantage, LLC

For John and Deirdre

Contents

12 An integrated theory   93

    Appendix   97
    Index   109

Foreword

In introducing Sarah Nettleton's indispensable book, I would like to start with a personal reminiscence.

My acquaintance with Bollas goes back to the late '70s when, invited by Adriano Giannotti and Andrea Giannakoulas, he would come every six months or so as visiting professor to the renowned Istituto di Neuropsichiatria Infantile (as it was then called) at the University of Rome 'Sapienza'.

His visits were always an event. Many of the papers that were to be published later in *The Shadow of the Object* (1987) were presented in Rome for the first time, to an audience delighted by the crystalline transparency and clarity of his thinking, which was combined with great complexity. In the hall you could have heard a pin drop.

Those who, like me, would sit in the front row, could observe Bollas's expression during the consecutive translation. In that brief interval between the previous phrase and what he would say next, one sensed that Bollas was spontaneously rethinking, then and there, continually coming up with new clinical and theoretical ideas. It was as if we were seeing, *in statu nascendi*, a surge of creative thinking. Sometimes he would apologize for contradicting something he had just said: he had rethought it as the translator was speaking, and a more convincing formulation had come to mind. It was always a work in progress.

In individual supervision I had a similar experience: Bollas had an unparalleled capacity for listening (even to my halting English), paying infinite attention to the precise phrasing of both patient and analyst. He would often ask to hear how the patient had expressed himself in Italian, and exactly how I had responded. The way in which each unique unconscious speaks has continued to be a central theme in his work.

Many contemporary psychoanalysts have developed, often very productively, the ideas of the great psychoanalytic figures of the last half century. However, Bollas's creativity is of a different order. Although he takes up ideas from others – Freud, Winnicott, Bion – the core of his work is completely and indisputably the result of his own clinical and theoretical thinking. In my view, no author within contemporary psychoanalysis has the same originality of thought. As we say in Italian: '*è farina del suo sacco*'.

He is immensely prolific; there is hardly time to finish reading one book before the next one comes along, taking the reader down unexpected pathways that may have little or nothing to do with the preceding work, but which are invariably characterized by his unique style of writing. He has produced what can seem like a bewildering plethora of ideas, and he has never offered a systematic organization of his own conceptualizations of psychoanalysis. However, the evolution of his thought presents a highly complex theory of unconscious life.

Nettleton's work organizes the fundamental elements of this theory into chapters that enable the reader to grasp the structure of Bollas's metapsychological thinking. It is an accomplishment of remarkable lucidity, focus and integration, and in fulfilling this task – one that no one else has had the courage to tackle – she has rendered a unique service to the reader. She combines a modest style (never imposing her own ideas on his) with admirably rigorous and accurate scholarship that demonstrates her profound grasp of the most subtle nuances of his writing.

The architecture of the book, designed around continually expanding themes, renders Bollas's concepts enjoyably approachable for those who are encountering his ideas for the first time, but it also offers to his aficionados a valuable opportunity to deepen their understanding.

Vincenzo Bonaminio

Preface

I encountered the work of Christopher Bollas in 1987 when I read his first book, *The Shadow of the Object: Psychoanalysis of the Unthought Known*. At that time my relationship with psychoanalysis was embryonic, and, looking back, I am sure that I understood very little of what the book was saying. But something about it caught my attention. I have since discovered that this is a common experience – for many people, Bollas's writing resonates with something subliminal, hard to pin down.

Both my family background and my first profession as a musician rooted me in the arts, and it was perhaps because of this that I was drawn from the start to the British Independent Group, both to their questioning ethos and to a particular inclusive breadth in their psychoanalytic thinking. I was inspired by the illuminating work of writers such as Sharpe, Rycroft, Milner, Khan, Symington, Klauber and Coltart, but at the same time I was aware of an absence in Independent thinking of a theory of the mind that felt truly coherent.

I continued to read Bollas's psychoanalytical works as they appeared – *Forces of Destiny: Psychoanalysis and Human Idiom* (1989), *Being a Character: Psychoanalysis and Self Experience* (1992), *Cracking Up: the Work of Unconscious Experience* (1995), *The Mystery of Things* (1999), *Hysteria* (2000), *Free Association* (2002) and *The Freudian Moment* (2007). Then, in the late 1990s, it was my good fortune to be supervised by him for 18 months during my clinical training. By that time I had already been in supervision with a number of Independent analysts who had taught me a great deal about clinical work, but learning from Bollas turned out to be a unique and somewhat devastating experience. I felt the rug pulled out from under my feet. It was immediately clear that this was an approach I had not encountered before, and in those intense, eye-opening sessions I felt my understanding being transformed.

My involvement with his thinking gained an added dimension in 2004, when I became one of his editors. I worked with him first on his trilogy of novels – *Dark at the End of the Tunnel* (2004), *I Have Heard the Mermaids Singing* (2005) and *Mayhem* (2006) – and on his volume of dramatic works, *Theraplay and Other Plays* (2006). These were followed by *The Evocative Object World* (2009), *The Infinite Question* (2009), *The Christopher Bollas Reader* (2011), *China on the Mind* (2013), *Catch Them Before They Fall* (2013) and *When the Sun Bursts: The Enigma of Schizophrenia* (2015).

In 2009, aware that I had had a unique and privileged opportunity to immerse myself in Bollas's work, and keen to share my experience of this revolutionary psychoanalytic thinker, I devised a series of seminars that introduced and explored the fundamentals of his metapsychology. Since then I have taught many groups in the UK and in Oslo, Tel Aviv, Paris, Washington, New York and Istanbul. I have encountered an inspiring enthusiasm for his work, and I am immensely grateful to the seminar participants, who have continually challenged me to deepen and clarify my own understanding.

Acknowledgements

Extracts from Bollas's *The Freudian Moment* (2007) are reprinted with kind permission of Karnac Books. My thanks also go to Christopher Bollas for the quotations from *The Shadow of the Object: Psychoanalysis of the Unthought Known* (1987), *Forces of Destiny: Psychoanalysis and Human Idiom* (1989) and *The Christopher Bollas Reader* (2011); to Free Association Books for those from *Freely Associated: Encounters in Psychoanalysis* (ed. Molino, 1997); and to Routledge for extracts from *Being a Character: Psychoanalysis and Self Experience* (1993), *Cracking Up: The Work of Unconscious Experience* (1995), *The Mystery of Things* (1999), *The Evocative Object World* (2009), *The Infinite Question* (2009), *China on the Mind* (2013) and *Catch Them Before They Fall* (2013).

I am grateful to Kate Hawes at Routledge for her immediate enthusiasm for this project; to Ruth Harvey, Elizabeth Qabouq, Lois Oppenheim, Bruce Reis and Mary Twyman for their valuable comments on the manuscript; and to Vincenzo Bonaminio for his generous encouragement and for writing the Foreword.

And, most of all, my thanks to Christopher for giving us so much.

Abbreviations

When Bollas's writings are quoted in the text, his books will be coded as follows:

SO   *The Shadow of the Object: Psychoanalysis of the Unthought Known* (London: Free Association Books, 1987)

FD   *Forces of Destiny: Psychoanalysis and Human Idiom* (London: Free Association Books, 1989)

BC   *Being a Character: Psychoanalysis and Self Experience* (London: Routledge, 1993)

CU   *Cracking Up: The Work of Unconscious Experience* (London: Routledge, 1995)

MT   *The Mystery of Things* (London: Routledge, 1999)

FM   *The Freudian Moment* (London: Karnac, 2007)

EOW   *The Evocative Object World* (London: Routledge, 2009)

IQ   *The Infinite Question* (London: Routledge, 2009)

CBR   *The Christopher Bollas Reader* (London: Routledge, 2011)

CM   *China on the Mind* (London: Routledge, 2013)

CF   *Catch Them Before They Fall* (London: Routledge, 2013)

Introduction

Christopher Bollas has made an extraordinarily broad contribution to contemporary psychoanalysis. In addition to his work on theory, clinical technique and psychopathology, he has applied his understanding to fields such as literature, architecture, history and social anthropology, as well as to the politics of the psychoanalytic world and the issue of confidentiality.

Bollas grew up in California. He studied history at Berkeley and then began his clinical career in 1967, working for two years at a day centre for autistic and schizophrenic children in Oakland. There the principal theoretical influences were Anna Freud, Bruno Bettelheim and Margaret Mahler, but in his efforts to understand the severely disturbed children he was getting to know, he already found himself gravitating towards British psychoanalysis and the work of writers such as Klein, Winnicott and Tustin.

While studying for a PhD in English literature at the University of Buffalo, he pursued a training in psychoanalytic psychotherapy for non-medical graduate students. He then completed a qualification in social work at Smith College and was trained in ego psychology during his placement at Beth Israel Hospital in Boston.

In 1973 he moved to London, where he studied and worked at the Tavistock Clinic, both in the adult department where he was influenced in particular by Independent and Bionian analysts, and in the child and adolescent department where he studied with Francis Tustin, Donald Meltzer and Matte Harris. At the same time he trained at the Institute of Psychoanalysis, taking Classical Freudian, Independent and Kleinian seminars. There he was supervised by Paula Heimann, Marion Milner, Clifford York and Eric Brenman.

During this period he also became interested in French psychoanalysis, working with J.-B. Pontalis and André Green. For 20 years he was visiting professor of psychoanalysis at the University of Rome, where he lectured every two months, and for over 30 years he conducted workshops with groups of psychoanalysts in Sweden, Germany and the USA. He was a founding member of the European Study Group for Unconscious Thought.

Many people have read a few of Bollas's papers and are familiar with, for example, his concepts of the unthought known and the transformational object. To those of a certain turn of mind his writing is immediately appealing. He deals with creativity, aesthetic experience, the uniqueness of human character . . . rather alluring, feel-good ideas. But what is difficult to appreciate without a more thorough reading of his work is the intellectual rigour and the internal coherence of his thinking, which brings together theory and technique, normality and pathology, and offers a unique exploration of the complex interrelationship between private, internal, subjective experience and the world of external objects.

In many senses, Bollas's contribution belongs firmly within the British Independent tradition, expanding on themes that have concerned Independent writers since the early days of psychoanalysis in Britain. His thinking is also influenced by Kohut, Bion and Lacan, and, very significantly, by Winnicott's ground-breaking theories about the relationship between infant and mother, and his concept of the 'intermediate area' in the mind – the arena for creativity and imagination.

First and foremost, however, Bollas's work is based on a deep reading of Freud. In various crucial respects, he picks up on ideas that were part of Freud's *intuitive* vision which, partly because of the limitations of his own personality, Freud himself did not fully acknowledge or explore.

He also refers throughout his work to numerous extra-psychoanalytical influences, including Bachelard, Barthes, Melville, Camus, Ionesco, Heidegger, Derrida, Mahler, Kant and de Kooning. In an interview with Anthony Molino, he says:

> I think de Kooning's way of painting captures something about the nature of the unconscious; there's something about his expression of textures, of thought and ambition and endeavor, and about the way he erases . . . The way he scrapes off certain lines, certain figurations that are then painted over . . . but the erased lines are still there somewhere . . . Something about his vision, his vision and re-vision, really spoke to me. What he taught me, in a way similar to Freud's theory of deferred action, is that the unconscious is not just an envisioning, but a re-visioning; and therefore, while one is writing one's self, one also edits and cuts and pastes and reviews, again and again and again.[1]

This unusually broad range of influences has led Bollas to a committed espousal of theoretical plurality. In relation to this, it is a matter of regret to him that (thus far at least) he has not explored in detail the world of Jungian thought. My seminars on his work have attracted many Jungian colleagues, and it has been interesting to discover that they often feel more easily at home with certain aspects of Bollas's thinking than those trained in the Freudian tradition. In fact, I believe that his work has the potential to provide a much-needed link between these two worlds, sadly driven apart by historical antipathies.

Bollas's written style is personal and distinctive. In his early books especially, we see the legacy of his former life as an academic. The writing is frequently dense, including many references to literature and philosophy, and his argument can at times seem dauntingly complex. However, passages of extreme condensation will typically alternate with anecdotes from his life or other examples from the everyday, producing a balance between refined abstract concepts and ordinary human experience, and enabling the struggling reader to resituate himself in the familiar. At times we encounter an intriguing phenomenon: his writing embodies what he is describing. As we engage with his words we do not simply acquire intellectual ideas; we find ourselves *experiencing* something about our own internal world.

His language itself can be idiosyncratic. He may use a common word in an uncommon way – 'processional' refers to a process rather than to a procession – and if he cannot find a suitable word for what he wants to express, he will happily invent a new one. Terms such as 'ghostline personality', 'normotic illness' and 'interformality' are testament to the innovative creativity of his thinking, and these neologisms often represent his most imaginative pushing of conceptual boundaries.

For Bollas, psychoanalysis is no ivory tower. Although at times his concepts may seem rarefied, his thinking deals with lived experience. As well as creating a continuum between normal human subjectivity and the various manifestations of psychopathology, he extends the language of psychoanalysis into many aspects of society and culture. He offers an overarching model of psychic structure and functioning, but he also puts into words the intense minutiae of life: a wisp of a thought, an elusive fragment of self-experience. He gives us ways to think about what it is like inside our head, but he never loses sight of what is ultimately unspoken and unreachable in the self.

A chronological reading of Bollas's works suggests that his picture of the mind was present, in essence, from the beginning of his writing. However, his metapsychological model does not appear as a whole in any one place. This creates a problem for the reader. It can be difficult to track down papers on particular topics, and it is easy to miss out on essential concepts. In my seminar groups I have often encountered fervent enthusiasm for his work coupled with a lack of understanding of the fundamentals of his thinking.

The present book is an attempt to remedy this situation. It is designed to be a guide, a sort of route map, that will enable the reader to grasp the theories that underpin Bollas's model. It is not intended as a critique, a comparative study or a comprehensive introduction to the whole of his work. For the reader who is interested in other areas of his writing, the Appendix provides suggested papers listed by topic.

Taking a thematic rather than a chronological view, the book provides a sequential introduction to the key elements of Bollas's metapsychology, and it is therefore designed to be read from start to finish. Although the various concepts are somewhat mutually dependent, they are introduced here in a linear fashion; ideas are not used as part of the discussion until they have been presented in themselves. Just as the mind develops from simplicity into complexity, the later chapters make use of the earlier concepts and are therefore more demanding. This cumulative approach is intended to illustrate the way in which the individual elements of his conceptual vocabulary come together to form an integrated theory.

The first chapter explores a dualistic principle that, in various forms, is a central theme throughout Bollas's work. We then embark on an exploration of the individual elements of his thinking: the receptive unconscious and psychic genera, idiom and the unthought known, self and character, the evocative object, unconscious complexity, free association and the Freudian Pair. The penultimate chapter explores his ideas about the diversity of approaches that exist within contemporary British psychoanalysis, and the final chapter acts as a coda in which the threads of his metapsychology are drawn together.

Chapters 2–11 begin with a note of key papers relevant to the topic and a list of key concepts. These build throughout the book to form a glossary of Bollas's psychoanalytic language.

I have synthesised material from various sources: his extensive writings, the experience of his clinical work gained in supervision, unpublished material that he has kindly allowed me to use, and many personal communications and discussions that have expanded my understanding, for which I am especially grateful.

Bollas's extraordinary work evokes a very personal response; it invites ramifying thought. Since I would like to leave readers free to pursue their

own inner responses, my aim has been to clarify rather than to interpret, but some of the illustrative examples, and certain emphases, are my own.
The map is no substitute for the journey. The book will have succeeded if its readers feel inspired to explore Bollas's work for themselves.

Note

1 Molino, A. (ed.) (1997) *Freely Associated: Encounters in Psychoanalysis.* London: Free Association Books, p.34.

Chapter 1

Psychic dualities

Underlying Bollas's metapsychology there is a fundamental polarity between two broad principles. This duality manifests in many different ways, including:

maternal	*paternal*
form	*content*
merged	*delineated*
intuitive	*conceptual*
receptive	*active*

We encounter these two modes from birth (probably in some form even before birth) and both remain within us, moment-to-moment, as potential forms of being. The balance, and the tension, between them influence all aspects of our intrapsychic life and underpin our encounters with the external world.

Bollas frequently alludes explicitly to the duality of the maternal and paternal orders.

During the primary phase of life within the maternal dyad, unconscious axioms of being and relating are absorbed by the infant as he exists within the experience of the mother's way of feeding, handling and relating to him.

As the child becomes verbal, and during the Oedipal phase, father, siblings, extended family and the wider world intervene and introduce him progressively to the existence of a reality outside the self, and to the objective structures and demands of society. He encounters the awareness of sexual difference, the primal scene and parental desire, the challenges of rivalry, and the need to communicate using a shared language.

This is life governed by the paternal order, which first announces itself in visceral ways that Bollas describes as follows:

> the "textural" difference of the father from the mother, or the "feel" of the father: the father who embodies a different odor, a different smell, who has a different way of holding, of carrying the child; who has a different way of breathing, of walking, a different tone of voice.[1]

Both at a sensory level and in the realm of thought and imagination, the duality embodied by the idiosyncrasies of maternal and paternal care forms a template for the existence of two distinct categories of experience.

Bollas describes the way in which maternal and paternal functioning come together in the psychoanalytic session with the process of recounting a dream. Whereas the dream is dreamt within a private, hallucinatory world, its reporting involves the dreamer in the attempt to capture it in words. The patient is asked to transform something private, evocative and imbued with emotional subtlety into a verbal communication with an external other. However, Bollas points out that the psychoanalytic approach to understanding a dream involves both modes of experience:

> the requirement is remarkably laid-back: simply say what is on the mind in association to the dream. The analyst does not interrogate the patient or demand that the patient make sense of the dream. Instead the patient lingers with the dream text, borrowing from its form, and talking without knowing much of what this means, rather like the dreamer inside his or her own dream. But as time passes and the analysand follows different lines of thought, the unity of the dream seems to break down and the associations take the dreamer very far away from the dream experience [. . .] That oracular aspect of the dream – the maternal oracle that held the dreamer inside it, spoke in the dreamer's ear, brought visionary events before the dreamer's very eyes – is displaced by the dreamer's own mental life.[2]

Although the externalising process of conveying the dream in words can be understood to represent the intrusion of paternal demands into the maternal idyll, Bollas considers that the analysis of the dream 'accomplishes a mature pairing of the internal mother and father, and leads to *an unconscious integration of the maternal and paternal orders in the analysand*'.[3]

In his book *China on the Mind* he explores this duality on a grand
scale, in terms of the contrast, both of culture and of intrapsychic structuring, between Eastern and Western traditions.
Western language and thought are characterised by delineated parts
of speech with different functions, making a clear distinction between
subject and object and allowing precision and organisation. They are
governed, therefore, by the paternal order. Eastern civilisations, and specifically those branching out from Ancient China, are rooted by their
spoken and written language in the holistic and the maternal. The Chinese character consists of a pictorial cluster of associations that combine
to convey inherently complex meanings that will resonate differently for
each person. Bollas writes:

> Eastern discourse is ambiguous, allowing for communication to
> be co-constructed, whereas Western discourse favours lucidity and
> a clear distinction between speaker and recipient. The message is
> thus an indicator of *difference*, an act that separates and demarcates
> people from one another.[4]

Western thinking is causal, metonymic, diachronic; Eastern thinking is cor-
relative, metaphoric, synchronic. 'The Chinese examined the world in the
differing forms of its process, rather than in its substantive differences.'[5]
Whereas early Western literary texts were concerned with the adven-
tures of the individual in the external world, the East focused on evanes-
cent moments of ordinary life, and the connection between the inner self
and the universal soul of man. Western heroism is set against Eastern
introspection and transcendence:

> Both East and West regard human life as a journey, but they dif-
> fer in their understanding of this. The Western mind explores the
> material world, discovering new evidence in a never-ending journey
> that honours its adventurers, who are identified with the found. The
> emphasis is on a venture that penetrates the real, analyzes and orga-
> nizes it, and presumes to add to the pool of knowledge. The Eastern
> mind explores the spiritual world, discovering new internal posi-
> tions that a self can take in order to instantiate through heightened
> consciousness ever more inspired forms of the immanental.[6]

During this exploration of Bollas's metapsychology we shall encounter
these dualities repeatedly, represented by various pairs of concepts: the
repressed and the receptive unconscious, psychic genera and psychic

trauma, focus and dissemination, self presentation and self representation, subjective and objective modes of thought, and the significance for our clinical understanding of the interplay between form and content.

Notes

1 Molino, A. (ed.) (1997) *Freely Associated: Encounters in Psychoanalysis.* London: Free Association Books, p.21.
2 Bollas, C. 'Free association', EOW p.44.
3 Bollas, C. 'Psychic transformations', FM p.10 (original italics).
4 Bollas, C. *China on the Mind*, p.4.
5 Ibid.
6 Ibid., p.6.

Chapter 2

The receptive unconscious and psychic genera

Key papers

'What is theory?' (FM)
'Psychic genera' (BC)
'Psychic transformations' (FM)
'Articulations of the unconscious' (FM)

Key concepts: *repression and receptivity; unconscious perception, unconscious creativity and unconscious communication; the receptive unconscious; psychic genera*

In the current political climate, the psychoanalytic profession is increasingly called upon to define itself, and one of the ways in which it may seek to do this is by claiming a unique therapeutic concern with the unconscious.

But the question arises: what sort of unconscious do we mean? How do we imagine the unconscious, and the role it plays in the structure and functioning of the mind? This question may threaten one of the few areas of assumed cohesion in the psychoanalytic world, but it has crucial implications for our understanding of all aspects of psychoanalysis: its theories, its clinical approaches and its therapeutic aims.

In this chapter we shall explore Bollas's theory of *the receptive unconscious*, which is, in my view, the most comprehensive and coherent contribution to the psychoanalytic understanding of the unconscious mind since Freud.

In 'What is theory?' (FM), Bollas sets out his problem situation – his rationale for producing a new metapsychological model – and he highlights various anomalies in Freudian theory. Freud offered three entirely different theories about mental structure. His topographical model was a spatial metaphor: the psyche formed in layers, with the conscious mind on top, the preconscious in the middle, and the unconscious out of sight below the surface.

Where did this model come from, and what does it enable us to understand?

Freud's early explorations in clinical psychoanalysis were centred around the problem of hysteria, and this led him to form a theory that privileged a certain aspect of mental functioning. In terms of psychic structure, he maintained in his early writings that the deepest, most fundamental part of the mind is the primary non-repressed unconscious, made up of the primitive physiological links between body and mind as well as our phylogenetic inheritance (nowadays we would probably call this our DNA). As the psyche develops, to this is added the repressed unconscious, consisting of material that has been banished from conscious awareness.

In Freud's work with Breuer, he made the revolutionary discovery that hysterical conversion is caused by repression: traumatic ideas that are unacceptable to the ego are pushed down into the unconscious, allowed to reappear only if they are disguised, often in the form of somatic symptoms. In the course of psychoanalytic treatment what has been forgotten is restored to consciousness, and this brings relief from the build-up of internal pressure that produced the physical manifestation. For thinking about hysteria the topographical model is entirely appropriate, and it invites a clinical focus on the re-emergence of repressed contents.

This model proposed that both the activity and the contents of the unconscious mind were governed by the repression of forbidden thoughts. However, in 1923, in *The Ego and the Id*, Freud encountered a theoretical problem. He had previously maintained that the unconscious *consisted* of repressed ideas, but he now realised that the agency that does the repressing is itself unconscious. So how was the unconscious to be defined?

This led him to propose his structural theory – a completely different metapsychological metaphor. Whereas the earlier model has concrete, spatial implications, this has an anthropomorphic flavour: it involves three parts of the mind with very different characters – id, ego and superego. This theory enables psychoanalysts to conceptualise a range of new issues. In particular, it offers a way of thinking about intrapsychic conflict in terms of a dynamic struggle between three agencies with incompatible aims. It allows a symptom to be considered, not just as a reaction to repressed ideas, but as the result of the play of opposing forces within the self. The structural theory also provides a conceptual vocabulary with which to approach the crucial issue of psychic development – something that cannot be approached using the simple model of conscious, preconscious and unconscious – and it highlights primitive relationships and Oedipal elements in the clinical situation.

It is important to note here that Freud's new formulation did not *replace* the old one. In the same way that Einstein's discoveries do not invalidate Newton's, the two theories simply address different issues. The theory of relativity came about because Einstein asked himself a new question about the speed of light, and Freud produced his structural theory when he realised that there were important aspects of unconscious functioning that could not adequately be described with the simple topographical model.

In fact, however, more than 20 years earlier Freud was already proposing another alternative model of the unconscious. In *The Interpretation of Dreams* (1900), he shows that dreaming, clearly a quintessentially unconscious process, is an astonishingly complex creative activity. Bollas describes the dreamwork as follows:

> Here the unconscious is an intelligence of form. Its proprioceptive capabilities receive endopsychic data from the storehouse of the unconscious; it also registers 'psychically valuable' experiences of the day, sorting them as the day goes on into a kind of pre-dream anteroom, and then it organises thousands of thoughts, arriving through the intermediate space of lived experience, to be dreamed. The creation of the dream is not only a remarkable aesthetic accomplishment, it is the most sophisticated form of thinking we have. A dream can think hundreds of thoughts in a few seconds, its sheer efficiency breathtaking. It can think past, present, and imagined future in one single image and it can assemble the total range of implicit affects within the day experience, including all ramifying lines of thought that derive from these experiences.[1]

It is clear that the unconscious that does the dreamwork is neither a primitive physiological unconscious nor one whose activity is confined to the mechanisms of repression and symptom formation, or conflict and defence. Bollas points out that neither the topographical nor the structural model enables us to conceptualise the *unconscious creativity* implied by dreamwork. However, when he explored accounts of the creative process given by artists, composers and scientists, he found striking parallels with Freud's theory of the dreaming unconscious. He also notes that in considering the 'day residue' as a central component of dream formation, Freud is presupposing a central role for *unconscious perception*, something missing from the model of an unconscious concerned solely with repression.

Throughout our waking life we receive, both from the external world and from our own bodies and minds, a constant stream of complex, interrelated impressions, both conscious and unconscious. Some of these will create internal conflict and will therefore be repressed as ego-dystonic. Most, however, will be details of the day that enter our mind without registering in consciousness simply because our attention is elsewhere. They thus become part of our internal world *without having been repressed*.

Freud acknowledges the existence of such unconscious perceptions:

> Everything that is repressed must remain unconscious; but let us state at the very outset that the repressed does not cover everything that is unconscious. The unconscious has the wider compass: the repressed is a part of the unconscious.[2]

However, he dismisses the importance of these other ingredients, regarding them as merely 'descriptively unconscious', psychically inert, with no role to play in the internal dynamics of the mind.

Another aspect that was recognised but left untheorised by Freud is the phenomenon of *unconscious communication*. In 1912 he writes: 'the doctor's unconscious is able, from the derivatives of the unconscious which are communicated to him, to reconstruct that unconscious which has determined the patient's free associations,'[3] and in 1915: 'It is a very remarkable thing that the *Ucs.* of one human being can react upon that of another, without passing through the *Cs.*'[4]

The constrictions of his materialist philosophy may have discouraged Freud from exploring such apparently numinous phenomena. However, Bollas proposes an additional reason why he might have failed to take up the issues implied by his theory of dreamwork. He notes that unconscious communication is present from the beginning of life, rooted in the preverbal attunement that exists between a baby and an ordinary devoted mother, and he suggests that Freud failed to recognise the fundamental creativity of the unconscious because, ironically enough, he repressed his knowledge of its generative, maternal aspects. He therefore left largely untheorised the earliest stage of development, when the infant lives within the maternal order, privileging instead the authority of the paternal in an account of psychic development based on superego castigation and censorship. Thus repression took centre stage, and the concept of unconscious receptivity was discounted.

Bollas goes on to wonder why these areas also tended to be glossed over by post-Freudian theorists, and he suggests that this may have been partly because a confusion arose involving the relationship between the topographical and structural models.

Following the appearance of the structural model, the topographical unconscious became identified with the id, and therefore came to be equated with the primitive part of the mind that the ego struggled to master and tame.

However, the equating of the unconscious with the id is a crucial mistake. Although the unconscious does house the most primitive elements of the mind, dreamwork shows that it also includes the most sophisticated elements. The infinite complexity of thinking that creates the dream and, as Bollas demonstrates, also underlies our everyday subjectivity, presupposes unconscious processes that have their own very active intelligence.

So Freud left us without a coherent theory with which to address some highly significant aspects of unconscious functioning, notably the phenomena of *unconscious perception, unconscious communication* and *unconscious creativity*. Whereas Freud claimed that repressed ideas were the only dynamic contents in the unconscious, Bollas suggests that other motivations and mechanisms are not only present but crucial to the growth of the mind and the development of the self:

> although the repressed unconscious is one important theory of unconscious thinking it is far too narrow a perspective and does not accord with Freud's theory of dreamwork, which is a theory of unconscious creativity. Our minds are far too complex to be about any one thing, be it a repressed idea, an id derivative, the transference, or anything. Indeed, at any moment in psychic time, if we could have a look at the unconscious symphony it would be a vast network of creative combinations.[5]

He therefore proposes a new metapsychological model, in which the building blocks of the psyche include both repressed ideas and those that are invited and received into the unconscious for creative reasons. He calls this *the receptive unconscious* or, elsewhere, *the received unconscious*.

In his third book, *Being a Character*, Bollas describes the mechanism by means of which the unconscious mind grows and is structured via a process of creative receptivity. This is his theory of *psychic genera*, in which he expands upon two Freudian concepts: 'thing-presentations', or preverbal experiences of things-in-themselves, and 'nodal points', at which different threads of psychic intensity converge in the unconscious.

From a linguistic point of view, the use of the word *genera* as both a singular and a plural noun takes some getting used to. Bollas acknowledges this, explaining that it was simply the best word he could find to refer to something with a dynamically changing structure that generates, gives birth to. He calls it 'a particular type of psychic organisation of lived experience that will result in creative new envisionings of life'.[6]

Psychic genera are matrices or clusters of internal intensity that are created when related ideas, images and feelings are attracted together with 'a collecting psychic gravity'.[7] As we experience the events of our lives, these matrices continually form and develop as new perceptions become linked into pre-existing clusters, forging connections between them and coalescing into an unconscious network of ever-increasing complexity. Psychic genera also communicate with the conscious mind. Bollas writes that they 'are organised, dynamic, and representationally effective in consciousness'.[8] They generate a desire for further pleasurable experiences and they promote a seeking for external objects that will offer the possibility of transformation and growth. This reciprocal process – external perceptions entering the unconscious and genera directing attention outwards – develops the structure of the mind in ways that will be unique to each individual.

It may be helpful to give a simple example to illustrate this process.

Let us imagine that a baby is lying in his cot, alone and in a state of quiet reverie. His mother appears, smiles, says hello, and attaches to the rail a red mobile toy that moves around in a random pattern. The baby's attention is immediately caught by this, and various elements come together: the familiar, reassuring arrival of mother, an unexpected new object in his line of sight, a stimulating red colour, the unpredictable movements, and the pleasurable experience of his own physical response as his body expresses surprise and excitement.

The point here is that the various aspects of this new experience enter the unconscious and become significant, not because they are *repressed* but because they are *received* for creative reasons. Each of the individual elements will link in the baby's unconscious with a cluster formed from previous experiences. With each new event, these clusters expand and sponsor a desire for a renewal of pleasurable excitement. The baby will then search his external environment for more of the same – the reappearance of mother, other things that are red or that move in an exciting way, and so on. In addition, connections between the separate internal constellations will be created and strengthened, so that later experiences will carry subtle resonances of earlier ones. This brief episode has added to the complexity of the baby's unconscious by creating new associative links.

Bollas describes this process as follows:

> The received would initially be constituted out of thing impressions that congregate in the unconscious and draw to them further thing

presentations that form nuclei in the unconscious. They become condensations of thousands of experiences and as we live and think, in time, our mind grows. The receptive unconscious stores unconscious perceptions, it organizes them, and it is the matrix of creativity.[9]

This is Bollas's model of how we think. And, rather intriguingly, his description of interacting psychic clusters conjures a visual image that is very close to the physiological reality of brain cell activity. In contrast to Freud's repression theory, the receptive unconscious involves a fluid, to-and-fro movement between the internal and external worlds. It also highlights the specific effects on us of objects, an aspect on which we shall focus in Chapters 3 and 7.

Bollas does not disagree with Freud that there are also matrices in the unconscious that are traumatically constituted, as painful experiences produce areas of defensive repression. Trauma and genera are fundamental ego dispositions towards reality. In any individual they will always appear in combination, with a fluctuating balance between the two.

In 'Psychic genera' (BC), he highlights aspects of the character and function of both types of constellation. Damaging experiences collect into matrices of trauma that aim to protect the self from further impingement by minimising contact with the object world, creating confusion between reality and fantasy. They are concerned with binding the self's energy, blocking contact, breaking links and creating a sense of nothingness in preference to pain. They produce isolation because trust in the outside world is lost.

They result in forms of pathological functioning that are all too familiar to clinicians. These are people who gravitate towards the negative. Only bad experiences count. They cling tenaciously to grievances, and will habitually transform a potentially generative experience into something destructive. They unconsciously sabotage relationships and attack the mental creativity of themselves and others. This incites rejection, reinforcing their picture of the world as hostile.

In contrast, psychic genera are unconscious clusters that promote expansiveness and linking. They are formed out of 'the psychic incubation of libidinal cathexes of the object world'.[10] The word 'incubation' has an important resonance here. The perception that is received into the unconscious does not merely exist in a static state; as it becomes associated with other experiences it changes and develops, protected from the demands of consciousness as the foetus is protected in the womb. Psychic genera sponsor open-mindedness and exploration. They engender a creative view of reality, symbolically elaborated, as the self pursues enrichment and growth through its engagement with external objects.

Bollas summarises this as follows:

> the theory of repression points only to the banishment of the unwanted, and I am convinced that other types of ideas are invited into the unconscious. To complement the theory of repression, we need a *theory of reception* which designates some ideas as the received rather than the repressed, although both the repressed and the received need the protective barrier provided by the anticathexes of preconsciousness. But if the aim of repression is to avoid the censoring or persecutory judgements of consciousness, the aim of reception is to allow unconscious development without the intrusive effect of consciousness.[11]

He explores the subjective experience of the activity of genera, noting that both artists and scientists describe a preliminary stage in the creative process in which they experience an abstraction of the problem. Disparate aspects begin to gather together, played with at first in the mind's eye, and only later forming into a conscious shape or concept. This requires a state of receptiveness, a creative fluidity. With clear implications for the clinical situation, Bollas emphasises the central importance to any creative process, whether scientific, artistic or psychoanalytic, of waiting – tolerating the state of not knowing.

He also links the activity of genera to the concept of *intuition*. Although apparently immediate and effortless from the point of view of the conscious mind, he suggests that what we experience as intuition may in fact be the result of concentrations of unconscious generative thinking, hitherto protected from premature consciousness.

If we are to accept the receptive unconscious as a valuable metapsychological model, we should expect it to offer a way of thinking about the development of the mind and the self, to illuminate our understanding of psychopathology and health, and to contribute to the theory of therapeutic technique. In what follows, I hope to show that Bollas's metapsychology does indeed offer innovative concepts that enrich all these areas of psychoanalytic thought.

Notes

1 Bollas, C. 'What is theory?', FM pp.72–3.
2 Freud, S. (1915e) 'The unconscious', *The Standard Edition of the Complete Psychological Works of Sigmund Freud, ed. Strachey, J. (London: Hogarth) XIV* p.165.
3 Freud, S. (1912e) 'Recommendations to physicians practising psycho-analysis', *SE XII* p.115.

4   Freud, S. (1915e) 'The unconscious', *SE XIV* p.193.
5   Bollas, C. 'Psychic transformations', FM p.27.
6   Bollas, C. 'Psychic genera', BC pp.67–8, footnote.
7   Ibid., p.73.
8   Ibid.
9   Bollas, C. 'Psychic transformations', FM pp.27–8.
10 Bollas, C. 'Psychic genera', BC pp.67–8.
11 Ibid., pp.73–4.

Chapter 3

Idiom

Key concepts: *idiom; the transformational object; the aesthetic moment; fate and destiny; futures*

In the previous chapter we explored the receptive unconscious, the core of Bollas's metapsychological model, in which the growth of the mind takes place by means of a process of associative receptivity. Emotionally invested experiences register in the unconscious as matrices or clusters of interconnected impressions, feelings and fantasies. These interact dynamically with one another and also influence the self's involvement with the external world.

We shall now consider *why* a particular experience might be significant for the infant, introducing Bollas's concept of *idiom*.

He maintains that every individual arrives with an essential kernel of self: 'the psychic correlate of the human fingerprint'.[1] He describes this as follows:

> We have within us a sense of a nucleus that gives rise to our particular aesthetic in being. We have a sense of our own self-authorship, of something that is irreducible and that determines us.[2]

To refer to this kernel of self, he uses the term *idiom*. Like our physical fingerprint, we arrive with it as part of our identity. We can never alter it or lose it, and nobody else will ever have it. This 'nucleus of logic' generates the unique aesthetic that guides our idiosyncratic relationship with the world, the way in which we unconsciously approach our experience. Physiology dictates that we are born with certain innate predispositions, and one aspect of this is that babies are naturally orientated towards different sensory modes. They therefore vary considerably in the kinds of experience to which they react most strongly. Some infants might respond predominantly visually, their attention easily caught by colours and moving shapes. Others might be strongly auditory, becoming lost in the sound of a hoover, human voices or music. Others respond kinaesthetically, their mood transformed by rocking, jiggling or dancing in their mother's arms.

So infants naturally resonate with particular *forms* of experience. This is a theme to which Bollas returns again and again, and the issue of form is central to his concept of idiom. He writes:

> The idiom that gives form to any human character is not a latent *content* of meaning but *an aesthetic in personality*, seeking not to print out unconscious meaning, but to discover objects that conjugate into meaning-laden experience.[3]

In his early seminal paper 'The transformational object' (SO), he describes the development of idiom in the earliest phase of life. At this stage the infant's reality is governed principally by the way in which the environment responds to him, and in particular by the mother's capacity for attuned caregiving. The everyday acts of looking after her baby – feeding, cleaning, soothing, playing – may convey mutuality or disconnection, facilitation or impingement. In an extension of Winnicott's concept of the 'environment mother', Bollas suggests that these ordinary daily acts produce alterations in the baby's self state. The mother is therefore experienced by the baby as a *transformational object*. He writes:

> Before language, before the sharing of the image governed by words, all of us are in communion with the indistinct energy of the forms that shape our world. We do not see what 'it' is, which is why I have written that the mother is perceived as a process of transformation, as a 'transformational object'. She is the form behind the form of things.[4]

In 'The spirit of the object as the hand of fate' (SO), he elaborates this idea with his concept of the *aesthetic moment*. It is important to emphasise that he is using the word 'aesthetic' not in a narrow sense that implies artistic sophistication, but to refer to any experience of creative internal transformation. As the mother offers her baby objects that attract his interest and give him pleasure, she gives form to the infant's idiom. Bollas therefore regards the infant's experience of the mother's idiom of care as the earliest human aesthetic. Throughout our lives, this engenders the desire and the expectation that the experience will be rediscovered, as aspects of our idiom meet and resonate with elements of the outside world, placing us in subjective rapport with objects.

In order to achieve basic trust, the infant needs to feel not only that his instinctual urges – his hunger, passion and aggression – are contained, but also that his idiom, his unique subjectivity, is perceived, recognised and welcomed. The mother's deep knowing of her infant allows her to sense his interests, needs and wishes, and a crucial part of maternal provision is the instinct to offer the infant particular objects with which he will instinctively resonate:

> If the mother knows her infant, if she senses his figural intentions, his gestures expressive of need and desire, she will provide objects (including herself) to serve as experiential elaborators of his personality potential. In this way, she assists the struggle to establish self.[5]

Emotionally significant objects do not merely provide the infant with psychic contents. Their discovery develops ego structures that will negotiate the interaction of idiomatic wishes and the environment.

As the baby grows into a toddler, the range of potential objects expands. As he becomes verbal, the experience of transformation will acquire additional dimensions, and what happens at this stage will affect his unconscious expectations about the possibility of communicating his internal world and having his idiom understood.

If he is relatively stable and emotionally free, the young child will eagerly seek out objects that allow him to elaborate his idiom, enjoying the excitement of novelty and imagination. However, if he is struggling with emotional conflict the choosing of objects will become restricted. In terms of the model of the receptive unconscious, children who are governed by traumatic matrices will close off contact with the generative elements of the unconscious mind. Bollas writes:

> If a child feels that his subjectivity is held by some container, composed of the actual holding environment of parental care and subsequently the evolving structure of his own mind, then the subjectifying

of the world feels licensed, underwritten, and guaranteed. But if this right is not secure, then a child will feel hesitant to release the elements of self to their experiencings.[6]

The idea of an innate, individual aesthetic which drives the search for aspects of the external world that resonate with our idiom is central to Bollas's thinking. In 'The evocative object' (BC), he illustrates this by quoting two sculptors, Barbara Hepworth and Alexander Calder, both of whom wrote about their experiences of the creative process. Although they clearly had in common an impulse to create three-dimensional objects, the contrast between them illustrates the subtlety and individuality of the issue of idiom.

Hepworth describes how she acquired her instinctive sense of form by being driven, as a child, over the landscape of her native Yorkshire, absorbed by the physical movement over undulating hills and valleys. She was aware that as she grew into a sculptor, the internalisation of these early physical, spatial experiences produced a strong individual aesthetic in her work – rounded shapes, soft and curving, some on a monumental scale. In other words, the early evocative experiences that spoke so strongly to her particular idiom became established as psychic structures that went on to generate the characteristic form of her sculpture. She writes: 'The sensation has never left me. I, the sculptor, am the landscape.'[7]

Calder, on the other hand, describes his inspiration as stemming from the image of celestial bodies floating in space, viewed in relationship to one another and constantly in motion. This he refers to as 'the ideal source of form'.[8] He went on to produce kinetic sculptures, constructed from separate, related components suspended in a delicate balance. Constantly moving, they seem barely tethered to the ground.

What is important here is not the *content* – the subject matter of the sculptures – but the drive towards the expression of an intrinsic sense of *form* that reflects individual idiom. The two sculptors convey in their writing that certain features of the external world were, for them, always highly evocative. They were conscious that their artistic activity was linked essentially to early events in their lives that constituted what Bollas calls 'transformative self experiencings'.[9]

These examples illustrate how each individual is drawn to particular elements in external reality that feel connected to the core of the self. Provided the environment has been sufficiently facilitating, significant objects will be sought and creatively engaged with as we move through life, so that each individual becomes 'a privately evolved but structured culture'.[10]

Psychoanalysts have tended to focus more on the content of the patient's communications than on their form. Form is harder to put into words; because it is essentially unconscious, we struggle to find a conceptual vocabulary with which to talk about it. Bollas writes:

> When Freud theorized the unconscious ego, he got to something which had that kind of dense intelligence to it: something that really has to do with the aesthetic organization of the self, or with the self as an aesthetic organization.[11]

In the following passage from his book *Cracking Up*, he relates these ideas to the clinical situation, emphasising the highly individual nature of idiom:

> A psychoanalyst develops a separate sense for each patient, attuned to the analysand's precise intelligence of form, as the patient takes the analyst through a process that derives entirely from the patient's aesthetic in being. The patient educates the analyst's sensibility, moving him along logical pathways that the analyst now knows are ideological positions. The analyst comes to sense the basic assumptions peculiar to the analysand's being, out of which he develops a sense of his patient's idiom.[12]

However effective the insights produced by the analyst's interpretations, the patient's experience of the *form* of the analyst as a presence may (and sometimes may not) be transformational in itself. It is a common experience at the end of a successful treatment that, although the patient may have acquired a greatly enhanced conceptual understanding of the events and relationships in his life, he is left with very little memory of exactly what was talked about for all that time. What he does take away, however, is a profound sense of being known. His idiom has been received and intimately engaged with. Patients are often left feeling that their analyst knows them better than anybody else, and this bears witness to the depth of meaning connected with our formal experience of the object. This profound relationship has been predicated on the original maternal dyad (no longer in conscious memory) within a physical setting instinctively designed by Freud to mirror that early stage of life.

How does Bollas's concept of idiom relate to Winnicott's 'true self'?[13] They certainly have elements in common. Both refer to the core of the self as an inherited potential, and both recognise the importance of an early good-enough facilitating environment in enabling the person to be in contact with this core. In fact, in Bollas's early work he uses the terms 'true self' and 'idiom' more or less interchangeably, but as he develops his concept it acquires a significantly different flavour.

Winnicott's theory of the true self refers to an internal capacity for spontaneity; it is related to instinctual life and therefore to the id. He describes it as vulnerable and needing protection; it is too fragile to be allowed unmediated access to the outside world. The 'false self' therefore forms as a necessary defence that protects the true self from threat, as part of the ego's negotiations with external reality.

Bollas's concept, on the other hand, refers to something more robust. Although it may be restricted in its development, our idiom can never be impinged upon or damaged. It does not require protection; like our fingerprint, it simply *is*. Moreover, it comes with an innate drive to express and elaborate itself, so unlike Winnicott's true self, which must be sequestered for its own safety, it actively *seeks* interaction with the outside world.

This contact involves not a protective falseness but true creative engagement. Throughout our lives, we pursue our needs, wishes and interests through our selection and use of psychically significant objects in a constant to-and-fro interaction between our idiom, our immediate environment and the wider human culture. Psychic life therefore consists of our innate disposition meeting up with the external world.

The central importance that Bollas accords to the ongoing development of idiom raises another issue. Psychoanalysis has traditionally been preoccupied with the significance of memory and the past, and has tended to ignore the importance in our internal world of plans, hopes and imaginings about what is to come. Bollas suggests that as well as repression of memories, there can also be a repression of what he calls *futures*.

In 'The destiny drive' (FD), he highlights this element of forward movement with a distinction between the concepts of *fate* and *destiny*. He designates as fateful experiences those that are externally determined, unpredictable and outside the subject's control. This implies early impingement that restricts the freedom of the self and interferes with the capacity to live creatively. If a person is in the grip of neurotic symptoms, fixations of character or psychosis, he can be described as fated. He lives in an internal world of self and object representations in which he will tend to repeat the same scenarios with little sense of potential or developing understanding. He feels helpless to influence his own life. Imprisoned by oppressive echoes of the past, the future feels devoid of hope. Early trauma, and in particular the loss of the primary object, can foreclose not only the future use of that object but also, crucially, the evolving articulations of the self that would have gone along with it. This brings an unconscious mourning for the loss of potential selves.

In terms of the receptive unconscious, this person will be governed by matrices of trauma, and will defensively reject links with the external world. If the early environment was not conducive to the expression and elaboration of his idiom, one of the tasks of an analysis will be to enable him to work his way out of these fateful entanglements so that he can move towards fulfilling his destiny.

Bollas's concept of destiny refers to a trajectory in the life of the individual towards the fulfilling of his unique potential. It implies self-determination, expansion and creativity, and it will be enabled in the early stages of development by parents who are attuned to the idiom of the infant. If we are free to pursue our destiny, our sense of future will be projected into fantasies, hopes and aspirations: visions of what may be to come in our life. The person who is in touch with his destiny has an expectation of progression; he can steer his own course. This endo-psychic projection gives him a sense of direction, fostering a passionate investment in objects and activities as he engages psychically with his future and works to create the conditions that will foster its fulfilment.

In some ways, Bollas's destiny drive and Freud's 'pleasure principle'[14] have similar connotations. However, the destiny drive implies something over and above instinctual satisfaction: it involves an aesthetic dimension and aim – the particular pleasure of the individual self in elaborating his idiom. Of course, even in the best of circumstances destiny is only ever partially fulfilled, and Bollas suggests that this may be the origin of the many theologies of an afterlife – be it heaven or reincarnation – that offer a promise of ultimate completion.

So the concept of idiom refers to the unique aesthetic in our personality that gives characteristic form to our intrapsychic dynamics and promotes a particular idiosyncratic engagement with the outside world, where it guides our object choices. In determining the kinds of experiences that resonate within us as valuable and significant, it has a key influence on psychic development.

In Bollas's metapsychology this concept has a radical implication: the centrality of the drive to express and elaborate our idiom suggests that the unconscious has a purpose. Idiom therefore displaces instinct as the nucleus of the mind. He writes:

> I do not propose that instinctual life does not exist. I simply do not give it that primacy that it holds for Freud. Somatic urges work all the time upon the mind. The drives of the id do demand expression,

a task performed by the ego. But each person organizes the id differently and this unique design that each of us is is more fundamental to the choice and use of an object than the energetic requirements of the soma which themselves express the idiom of the true self.[15]

Notes

1   Molino, A. (ed.) (1997) *Freely Associated: Encounters in Psychoanalysis.* London: Free Association Books, p.12.
2   Ibid., p.29.
3   Bollas, C. 'Being a character', BC pp.64–5 (my italics).
4   Bollas, C. *China on the Mind*, p.56.
5   Bollas, C. 'A theory for the true self', FD p.10.
6   Bollas, C. 'Being a character', BC p.53.
7   Hepworth, B. Pamphlet in the Barbara Hepworth Museum, St. Ives, quoted in 'The evocative object', BC p.39.
8   Calder, A. (1968) 'What abstract art means to me'. In *Theories of Modern Art*, Chipp, H. (ed.). University of California, Berkeley, p.561, quoted in BC p.40.
9   Bollas, C. 'The evocative object', BC p.40.
10 Molino, *Freely Associated*, p.7.
11 Ibid., p.8.
12 Bollas, C. 'A separate sense', CU p.37.
13 Winnicott, D. (1960) 'Ego distortion in terms of true and false self'. In *The Maturational Processes and the Facilitating Environment*. London: Karnac, 1990.
14 Freud, S. (1911) 'Formulations on the two principles of mental functioning', *The Standard Edition of the Complete Psychological Works of Sigmund Freud, ed. Strachey, J. (London: Hogarth) XII.*
15 Bollas, C. 'A theory for the true self', FD p.12, footnote.

Chapter 4

The unthought known

Key papers

'Being a character' (BC)
'What is theory?' (FM)
'Moods and the conservative process' (SO)
'The unthought known: early considerations' (SO)

Key concepts: *the unthought known; processional logic; moods; the conservative object*

We shall turn now to another crucial aspect of the child's reality as he develops within his environment, introducing what is perhaps Bollas's most widely recognised concept: *the unthought known.*

In 'What is theory?' (FM) he writes about the early evolution of the self within the primary maternal relationship:

> The unconscious formed between infant and mother and later toddler and mother, occurs, in Freudian theory, *before* the repressed unconscious. It is the era of the construction of the self's psychic architecture. Maternal communication – a processional logic – informs the infant's world view. What is known cannot be thought, yet constitutes the foundational knowledge of one's self: the "unthought known".[1]

Developing out of Freud's concept of 'thing-presentations', Bollas's theory of the unthought known refers to the infant's unconscious, learned assumptions about the nature of reality, based fundamentally on experiences that register in the mind before the advent of language.

In the earliest months, when the self is still enfolded within the maternal order, preconceptual knowledge about being and relating is absorbed by the infant from the ordinary experiences of daily life. As the mother feeds the baby, he takes in milk (content) but he also absorbs the particular nature and quality (form) of the experience that she provides. The term *processional logic* refers to the unconscious structure of the mother's idiomatic approach to caring for her baby and relating to him. He does not evaluate these processes of care; they are simply his reality. Bollas writes:

> The mother, for example, instructs the infant in countless axioms of being and relating presented through the logic of her actions. These actions are assimilated by the infant's ego to become formative paradigms that partly govern the infantile self.[2]

Let's consider an ordinary aspect of the everyday life of an infant, to see how experience becomes established as an unconscious assumption. We shall compare two different ways in which a baby might be woken up in the morning.

The first baby is asleep in her cot. Every day her mother comes into the room, opens the curtains and speaks to her brightly, with warmth and humour, communicating the expectation that being awake is exciting and fun. When the baby opens her eyes the mother picks her up, carries her across the room and talks to her enthusiastically about what they can see out of the window, encouraging her to engage with the outside world.

The second baby is also sleeping. His mother tiptoes quietly into the room. Leaving the curtains closed, she sits next to the cot and very lightly strokes the baby's head. He gradually emerges from sleeping into drowsiness, then, as he dreamily registers her presence and starts to move his limbs, she makes soothing, gentle sounds, waiting for him to let her know that he is ready for the day to begin.

These two ways of operating reflect very different maternal idioms. Neither is right or wrong, but for the two babies they will contribute to the formation of entirely different views of a certain aspect of the world. The transition from sleeping to waking creates in the infant unconscious assumptions about the experience of shifting self states, and templates such as this will influence related experiences throughout life. What happens at the start of each day will not be consciously remembered later, but these experiences will be profoundly formative. They become part of the unthought known – 'the self's psychic architecture'.

So the primary maternal relationship, involving the interplay between the infant's innate idiom and the unconscious logic of maternal care, provides the foundation of self experience. In 'Being a character' (BC), Bollas goes on to consider the subsequent period, in which the kernel of the infant's being begins to expand into a self within the life of the family as he takes his place amongst the complex dynamics of parents and siblings, all of whom will, of course, also be governed by their own unique combination of unconscious elements. He writes:

> I believe each of us at birth is equipped with a unique idiom of psychic organization that constitutes the core of our self, and then in the subsequent first years of our life we become our parents' child, instructed by the implicate logic of their unconscious relational intelligence in the family's way of being: we become a complex theory for being a self that the toddler does not think about but acquires operationally.[3]

So as the child grows, unconscious axioms about reality will be founded on many elements of the family's daily life, including mealtimes, bedtimes, parental moods, physical activity, approval and punishment. As the intrapsychic logic of the child's idiom meets the intersubjective logic of the family, these paradigmatic experiences grow into a continuously developing field of assumptions, rarely conceptually represented but immensely influential in governing his expectations of the world.

What evidence might we encounter, later, of this crucial foundational era in the development of the self? Just as traces of the Big Bang still echo through the universe, the unthought known permeates and underpins our entire life. At certain moments clues arrive, and Bollas suggests that these are sometimes expressed through a particular form of self experience that we refer to as a *mood*. In 'Moods and the conservative process' (SO) he explores the nature of this ubiquitous but rather neglected aspect of our intrapsychic world, suggesting that moods have specific functions for the self.

They have a number of striking characteristics. They are unconsciously determined and cannot be conjured at will. They have their own temporality: we enter, and later emerge from, a mood rather as we do from a dream. A person can be 'in a mood', yet still be quite capable of dealing with ordinary life. Whether or not he attempts to express his mood in words, it will have an effect on the other, in whom it may evoke a particular sensitivity. We tend to feel that we should respect the boundaries of another's mood space, aware that it may be intrusive to comment on it. We are instinctively careful with the person, rather as though we are dealing with a young child, and indeed we may have the conscious thought that he seems to have regressed from his normal adult functioning into a more primitive state.

Bollas suggests that moods recreate particular elements of early unthought self experience including specific states of being. Some seem to be creatively valuable, even necessary to well-being: a part of the self withdraws into a generative autistic enclave in order to work through a complex internal task. Other moods are object related; they are intended to be witnessed. There may be an unconscious aim of influencing the other into providing something for the self. This constitutes not a generative withdrawal but a coercive interpersonal process that may offer a glimpse of a certain type of formative early relationship.

He highlights a specific kind of mood that has the purpose of encapsulating an aspect of the child's experience in order to preserve it. It acts as 'a mnemic container of a particular self state'.[4] He suggests that certain infantile events register in the internal world, not as an object representations but in the form of a specific sense of identity. If this is not linked with an object it will remain unsymbolised, and it therefore persists in the unconscious as a preserved experience that has never been transformed or modified. The mood allows it to be re-experienced directly in the form of a vivid being-state. He writes:

> the person will have an ongoing relation to these conserved states of self as much as to his represented objects. During that special state of being that allows for the release of the conservative object – in moods – the individual will remain in contact with that child self who endured and stored the unrepresentable aspects of life experience.[5]

Moods can therefore allow moments of unthought known experience to come to consciousness in the form of a subjective feeling that also communicates something of itself to the other. Inevitably, we bring our existential assumptions to every human encounter, but it is generally only in the psychoanalytic situation that these become an implicit, and sometimes explicit, focus.

Analyst and patient will know something of one another before they have thought what they know. This 'something' represents the interaction between two sets of assumptions and the mutual unconscious effects of idiom – an aspect that will be explored further in Chapter 6. At first, the patient's idiomatic use of the analyst may be based predominantly on mechanisms of projection, but gradually both participants begin to think the unthought known.

When the analyst encounters a patient who is pervaded by a mood, this brings with it a very particular atmosphere and can offer a direct experience of unthought elements in the internal world. In presenting a mood to the analyst, the patient may be recreating unconsciously an aspect of her early environment, thus allowing the analyst to experience for himself something that is very familiar to her.

Amongst other things, it will provide implicit evidence of the effects on the child of the mother's idiomatic form of intersubjective logic. Although it may appear pathological, this sort of enactment may represent an unconscious attempt by the patient to preserve an archaic intimacy. If the function of the mood is to preserve an element of the primary relationship, there may be a sense of contact with something crucial to the self. If this is the case, the attempt to analyse it can feel threatening and may be met with intense resistance. However, Bollas suggests that it offers an important opportunity:

> The conservative object has enormous therapeutic potential, precisely because of its essential character of preserving some disowned aspect of the child's true self, the moment of breakdown of the relationship with his parents and the fault in the parents' functioning as transformational objects. In the mood state the patient is available for potential transformation of what has primarily been mood experiencing into sentient knowing. As the analyst gradually perceives, identifies and addresses the mood, he is already functioning where the parents did not – as a transformational object.[6]

The transference involves a replaying of past relationships and will often include a representation of the child self. However, in 'The unthought known: early considerations' (SO), Bollas suggests that it may also constitute a new experience, in which elements of unconscious knowledge that have not previously been thought can emerge into consciousness.

Throughout our life, the conscious mind is underpinned by the unthought known. Its earliest roots lie principally in the axioms of the mother's way of doing things. Then, as the demands of the Oedipal phase disrupt the maternal dyad, and as compromises are negotiated between the infant's idiomatic impulses and the rules and assumptions of social reality, unthought knowledge continues to be formed.

As adults, all the aspects of life that we encounter in the course of a day are met with unconscious templates that reflect a unique combination of idiom and experience. Bollas writes: 'There is in each of us a fundamental split between what we think we know and what we know but may never be able to think.'[7]

Notes

1 Bollas, C. 'Articulations of the unconscious', FM p.34 (original italics).
2 Bollas, C. *China on the Mind*, pp.2–3.
3 Bollas, C. 'Being a character', BC p.51.
4 Bollas, C. 'Moods and the conservative process', SO p.110.
5 Ibid., p.112.
6 Ibid., p.114.
7 Bollas, C. 'The unthought known: early considerations', SO p.282.

Chapter 5

Self relationships

Key papers

'The self as object' (SO)
'What is this thing called self?' (CU)
'Mind against self' (MT)

Key concepts: *self states; normotic illness*

Having considered Bollas's foundational theories of idiom and the unthought known, we shall now move on to explore his concept of *self*.

In the Molino interview, he points out an inherent paradox. Our use of the word 'self' can imply a whole – it refers to our own being as distinct from the other – and we have, at least at times, a subjective feeling of unity. Existing alongside this, however, is a complex composite picture:

> this self that we are has many representations of itself, along with many representations of the object. In one day alone we go through many different self states, which by itself implies a plurality to our experience of our own being. And it's not an occasional plurality: it's a structure. We're fated to be multiple.[1]

In 'What is this thing called self?' (CU), he describes intrapsychic reality as consisting of a continuously moving experience of self, one that includes our relationship with internal objects.

Whereas Klein viewed internal objects as unconscious, phantasied embodiments of the play of primitive instinctual forces, Bollas's concept of psychic genera (his version of internal objects) is different and inherently more complex, presenting, as we have seen, an intricate interrelation between internal and external. Although each unconscious matrix retains a distinct character and presence in the intrapsychic world, genera are not fixed, circumscribed entities, but continually developing constellations of associations that create a dynamic internal environment. Bollas describes them as *'highly condensed psychic textures*, the trace of our encounters with the object world'.[2] We have a relationship – partly conscious, partly unconscious – to each of these matrices individually but also to the complex of inner constellations as a whole.

For Bollas, the self is made up of these interactive internal presences. He illustrates this by suggesting we think of a particular episode in our life – a moment from childhood, perhaps. This will comprise many discrete *forms* of memory, including elements that might be, for example, emotional, tactile, auditory, visual, narrative, relational, somatic, imaginary or symbolic. As we remember the incident these aspects coalesce and, despite its complexity, a complete inner sense of the event can flash into our minds in an instant, with the speed of a dream image. What we consciously recall is a particular self experience.

These intense, remembered psychic states can be associatively evoked in many ways: by a word or a name, a smell, a sound, a photograph, a chance encounter. As we accumulate innumerable experiences throughout our life, our sense of self grows, forming an ever-increasing network, and our unique psychic texture is shaped by the ingredients of these experiences.

Amongst the many clusters of meaning that exist within us, there will be one constellation that represents our experience of self. But can we say that we have a relationship with our self? This would seem to involve being both subject and object, both wave and particle.

As toddlers acquire language, they will usually talk to themselves out loud, especially when they are alone. In fact even the babbling of the infant, often interpreted as a means of self-soothing or the practising of vocal sounds, may well represent a purposeful talking to the self, albeit not yet in the form of words.

As we grow older we learn the convention of keeping this inner dialogue private, but as we go about our everyday life we are constantly objectifying the self, engaging in internal conversations that help us organise our days, play out imaginary scenes, and manage our shifting feeling-states and anxieties. Semi-consciously, we debate what to have for breakfast, whether to walk or take the bus; we weigh up internally whether to go to the cinema or have an evening at home. As we talk to our self – 'Why don't you get this done before you go out?', 'You really must make this chapter less confusing' – the internal voice carries identifications, especially with the parents, the people who first addressed us as 'you'. The nature of our intrapsychic relating therefore mirrors unconsciously our early relationships with the external world, combined with the complexities of idiom and unconscious phantasy. In 'The self as object' (SO), Bollas writes:

> Our handling of our self as an object partly inherits and expresses the history of our experience as the parental object, so that in each adult it is appropriate to say that certain forms of self perception, self facilitation, self handling and self refusal express the internalized parental process still engaged in the activity of handling the self as an object. Through the experience of being the other's object, which we internalize, we establish a sense of two-ness in our being.[3]

Freud realised one aspect of this self objectification with his theory of the superego, and psychoanalysis has been very concerned with the nature of the relationships between different parts of the self. However, Bollas suggests that the familiar tripartite structure of id, ego and superego does not allow us to conceptualise adequately the complexity of these intrapsychic negotiations.

Another aspect of the self as object concerns the child's developing awareness of the body. This involves a split: as the baby recognises her face in the mirror, she perceives the body as an external object. However, while the visible body plays its part in external, shared reality, there also exists another, intrapsychic version of the physical self. Private, subtle and nuanced, this is the scene of instinctual life. It is the erotic self, which inhabits a parallel existence – unseen, secret and inextricable from phantasy.

How might we think about the relationship between self and mind? It seems paradoxical to separate the two, and yet from the Oedipal phase onwards the child begins to realise that his mind is a distinct aspect of himself that he is increasingly expected to apply and control in many different ways. No longer shielded inside the maternal dyad, but faced with the paternal structuring of existence and the demands of the wider world, he also discovers that other people have minds and that these can be unpredictable and sometimes incomprehensible.

The mind therefore becomes an object for the self. It can contain disturbing ideas – it produces worry and shame; it attacks us with nightmares and intrusive, obsessional thoughts. However, it is also a place where significant understandings can be stored for safekeeping. It can even be a source of private delight.

In 'Mind against self' (MT), Bollas writes:

> What we see is an emerging rhythm of mindfulness, mindlessness, and mind objectified as an object of thought as the child moves

about, sometimes full of ideas but not thinking about the fullness, sometimes so caught up in something that they are not aware of even having a mind, and occasions when they are thinking very intently about something on their mind, or in the extreme, thinking about their mind and the way it serves up curiosities of thought.[4]

Our relationship with our mind develops throughout life in many different ways. Psychoanalysts have written about attacks on the mind, when thinking is cancelled out as a defence against intrapsychic trauma. Safety lies in being mindless.

However, there are other possible forms of mindlessness. In some traditions it is cultivated as a specific and elevated self-state, a peaceful nirvana that transcends noisy mental complexity. Bollas suggests that the absence of mind may also represent the opposite of simplicity:

> Mindlessness then may refer to a state of unconsciously informed being, when we are operating at so many differing, intersecting planes of ideation that no single train of thought could carry the dense dissemination. We are mindless not because nothing is happening inside but because too much is taking place for us to represent it.[5]

What about the puzzling, paradoxical forms of self that we experience in dreams? In 'The wisdom of the dream' (CBR), Bollas addresses the phenomenon of multiple dream selves. When we dream, one part of the self is represented as the experiencing self, while others might appear as characters in the drama. Dreams therefore constitute complex object relations, and in each individual they will tend to have a particular idiosyncratic flavour. Do the dreams include sexual desire? Is the dreamer constantly faced with tasks to perform? Do they involve anxious scenarios populated with menacing, persecuting objects? Are they typically bizarre and disconnected or do they present a lucid story?

Both night dreams and daydreams allow the subject to locate an objectified portion of himself within a script. The figure of the dreamer is like a double, an emissary from the world of the unconscious. As analyst and patient associate to the dream images and to the actions of the dreaming self, the dream is revealed as a rendezvous for parts of the self. Sometimes it will objectify a current life dilemma and may even supply an answer. It can seem then that the waking self and the dreaming self are working together. Bollas writes:

> The two aspects of the self are aware of one another. Indeed, I think it is proper for us to consider this a form of relationship. It is

intrasubjective, constituted out of two subjective positions – the night self and the day self – that are continuously interdependent throughout the lifespan and that seem to recognise their relative positions.[6]

What happens when the relationship with the self goes wrong?

In numerous clinical vignettes, Bollas addresses many varieties of self disorder, and these also serve to highlight particular aspects of the self's normal functioning. A person may, for example, lack an internal space for the reception of his own wishes or for the gratification of desire. Or he may lack the capacity for the mediation of conflict between wishes, inhibitions and external constraints. Some people live in a world of wish-fulfilling daydreams, rejecting engagement with the external. Although they are not psychotic, they habitually retreat into a parallel reality populated with imaginary characters, in which extended fantasy scenarios are played out, often over many years.

Some of Bollas's papers on psychopathology follow traditional diagnostic categories. Others identify new forms, such as 'The trisexual' (SO), 'The anti-narcissist' (FD) and 'The ghostline personality' (FD).

In his paper 'Normotic illness' (SO), he focuses on what happens if our idiom is severely inhibited. He coins the word 'normotic' to describe someone who is at the opposite end of the spectrum from the psychotic. Whereas a schizophrenic patient might retreat from reality into fantasy, the normotic person retreats from fantasy into reality in order to remove himself from subjective experience.

This is a person who is uninterested in, even mystified by, the idea of an internal world. Avoiding introspection, he is ruled by the objective; he deals in doing rather than being, and his days are arranged around schedules and activities. Although he has a persona in the external world, there is a sense that the self is unborn. Bollas writes: 'What is lacking is that originating subjectivity which informs our use of the symbolic.'[7]

This person will usually have been brought up in a stable, loving way. However, although his childhood contained no obvious trauma, adequate material care masked a subtle but crucial deprivation: the parents were unable to be alive to the communication of the infant's idiom. This meant that the *category* of internal reality was never securely formed and the imaginative life of the child went unrecognised and uncelebrated. Above all, this type of family prioritises conventional normality; activities take the place of living from the core of the self. Bollas summarises this situation as follows:

> some persons are abnormally normal. They are unusually rooted in being objective, both in their thinking and in their desire. They

achieve a state of abnormal normality by eradicating the self of subjective life, as they strive to become an object in their own being.[8]

In fact, normotic people are by definition extremely unlikely to seek analytic treatment, as they generally have no awareness of what they lack. However, the psychoanalyst is faced rather frequently with patients who complain of feeling empty. They may explicitly describe, or unconsciously convey, a sense that they have no self.

In 'What is this thing called self?' (CU), Bollas suggests that in trying to understand the apparent absence of self, it is instructive to note what has *not* been lost. The person has not lost his idiom; it is evident that he retains his essential identity – he is still unquestionably himself. It is also clearly different from the psychotic situation of losing the mind – he is aware of having mental contents and he knows that he is thinking, feeling and dreaming. And although his sense of agency may feel depleted, he is not without an ego. He is still using the operational part of the mind to perform the ordinary tasks of life.

So what is it that is missing? Although in most respects the person is still *operating* as a self, it seems that he does not *perceive* from his inner psychic processes a sense of the presence of the self. He is out of contact with his guiding inner logic; he has lost his relationship with the forming intelligence that lies behind the practical capabilities of the ego. It seems that the self is not merely the sum of its parts – those discrete aspects that we can reflect upon. It involves our *awareness* of our individual aesthetic intelligence. This provides us with a place to be, internally, and it can be a terrifying experience if it is not there.

As we know, the most radical disruption of self happens in psychotic illness. In 'Mind against self' (MT), and most extensively in *When the Sun Bursts: The Enigma of Schizophrenia* (2015), Bollas discusses psychosis from the point of view, not of mental contents, but of the structure of the relationship between self and mind.

Under normal circumstances, when something causes us to reflect, this draws attention to the mind as an object that needs to be engaged with. We create a temporary bifurcation in order to clarify our understanding before our self experience comes together again. Throughout a normal day, we oscillate between states of calm mindlessness and moments of focus and internal debate.

In psychotic illness, however, the mind can become irrevocably separated from the experiencing self, often manifesting as a disembodied voice that controls the self with imperious commands. This can turn into a powerful, secret relationship with an internal conspirator. As the mind is increasingly felt to be a threat, the person will try to avoid contact with it, and the widening gulf between mind and self now becomes the seat of the problem. These patients suffer profound anxiety about the mind, and in a therapeutic situation they can experience great relief at the opportunity to think about it as an object with someone who is not alarmed by it.

So what can we conclude about the meaning of the term *self*? It will be clear that for Bollas it is a highly complex issue. He writes: 'in the word "self" we have found the word that contains the highest degree of the unthought.' [9] In 'Being a character' (BC), he brings us back to the dense complexity of internal experience, describing it as follows:

> Our inner world, the place of psychic reality, is inevitably less coherent that our representations of it; a moving medley of part thoughts, incomplete visualizations, fragments of dialogue, recollections, unremembered active presences, sexual states, anticipations, urges, unknown yet present needs, vague intentions, ephemeral mental lucidities, unlived partial actions: one could go on and on trying to characterize the complexity of subjectivity, and yet the adumbration of its qualities does poor service to its reality.[10]

From a theoretical point of view, we can conceptualise the self in various ways: as the sum of internal representations, as the object of an internal dialogue, or as a conglomeration of shifting self states. The self has a presence in the real, yet it will always evade our grasp. In this sense it is analogous to the dream: existing as a circumscribed entity, yet with meanings that disseminate, potentially for ever, in innumerable directions. It is both a unity and an infinite network.

In the introduction to *The Shadow of the Object*, Bollas writes:

> Over a lifetime we objectify, know and 'relate to' the many different states in our being. Emotional and psychological realities bring with them self states which become part of our history. The concept of self should refer to the positions or points of view from which and through which we sense, feel, observe and reflect on distinct and separate experiences in our being.[11]

Notes

1 Molino, A. (ed.) (1997) *Freely Associated: Encounters in Psychoanalysis.* London: Free Association Books, p.29.
2 Bollas, C. 'Being a character', BC p.59 (original italics).

3   Bollas, C. 'The self as object', SO p.51.
4   Bollas, C. 'Mind against self', MT p.86.
5   Ibid., p.79.
6   Bollas, C. 'The wisdom of the dream', CBR p.254.
7   Bollas, C. 'Normotic illness', SO p.141.
8   Ibid., p.156.
9   Bollas, C. 'What is this thing called self?', CU p.176.
10 Bollas, C. 'Being a character', BC pp.47–8.
11 Bollas, C. 'Introduction', SO pp.9–10.

Chapter 6

Character and interrelating

Key papers

'Being a character' (BC)
'Character and interformality' (CBR)

Key concepts: *self presentation and self representation; interformality*

Having examined some of the complex internal relationships that coexist within the self, we shall consider now what happens when two selves meet.

Bollas uses the term *character* to refer to the form in which we unconsciously communicate with, and are received by, another person. He describes it as 'the pattern of being and relating generated by the idiom of each person's self'.[1]

This is one of the occasions when he takes a word in common usage and ascribes it an idiosyncratic meaning. In doing this he is generally highlighting a very specific aspect of our internal world, and in this case it is one that is relatively little considered by psychoanalysis. His interest in the concept of character as something that has an impact on the other reflects his academic background in the realm of literature. He points out that plays and films deal centrally with the simulation of character and its effects.

Whatever our individual intrapsychic complexities, and however out of touch with ourselves we may sometimes feel, each of us has some sense of internal familiarity. However, when we are confronted with the outside world's *impression* of us – if we hear a recording of our voice, and especially if we see ourselves on film – we are faced with ourself as an external object. It can come as a considerable shock to realise that this disconcertingly unfamiliar being is what the world is perceiving every day. It seems that there is a disconnection between our conscious awareness of ourself and the unconscious *effect* we have on the outside world.

Rather counterintuitively, Bollas suggests that we can never know our own character, although to others it is readily observable in the way that we interact with our objects. He relates this essential personal atmosphere to the idiom of an artistic work. It is a commonplace but nonetheless striking phenomenon that we can turn on the radio and recognise a composer from a few bars of music, even if we have not heard that particular piece before. The same can apply to looking at a painting or reading a poem. The idiom of the composer, artist or poet is conveyed by the characteristic *form* of the work, irrespective of specific content or subject matter.

Any encounter with another self is highly complex. Let us imagine we arrive at a dinner party. We are close friends with the host and we know some of the guests, but there are others whom we have not previously met. To the encounter with the familiar people we bring the totality of our shared history – activities, mutual friends, past conversations, varying degrees of conscious attraction, empathy or suspicion, and an intricate network of unconscious associations. With those who are new to us there may be no such historical background, but we are nevertheless struck immediately by an *impression* of each person, something that would be impossible to put into words. Before we experience anything they say or do, their presence has an effect on us.

Of course our response will inevitably include our own projections. The theory of projective identification allows us to think about an important aspect of a human encounter: one person receives and holds a split-off, projected part of the other, and the two are unconsciously assigned different roles. However, Bollas suggests that this familiar concept can be used too simplistically. He writes: 'the density of any person's being and their axioms of relating are too complex to be understood simply as discrete and discernible projections or role representations.'[2]

The impact of character relates to an intriguing variable in the clinical situation, one that also involves the enigma of unconscious communication. As the patient talks about himself and his experiences, the analyst develops a *sense* of the people in that person's life. These internal impressions may be vivid or elusive. With some patients we quickly form a distinct impression of their friends, colleagues and family members – sometimes we even feel we would recognise them if we met them in the street – whereas with others our picture remains permanently hazy.

In 'Being a character' (BC), Bollas explores the issue of idiom and communication in terms of form versus content. When we talk to a friend about our experience of a third person, he suggests that we evoke the feel of that person, not merely with the words we choose to describe them, but also unconsciously, via the *form* of our communication. He writes:

> I can talk to my analyst about my father, but what happens over time is that he will know him less through the precise contents of the associations than through some intriguing effect upon himself which gathers into his inner experiencing something of the nature of what I hold within myself.[3]

People vary greatly in their degree of permeability. Unconscious communication of the idiom of the other involves the recipient being, as Bollas puts it, *in-formed* by it. The roots of this capacity are related to the infant's experience of the mother's receptivity to her baby, beginning with her primary maternal preoccupation – her ability to be absorbed. Bollas maintains that if the analyst is to be receptive in this way he needs to empty his mind so that unconscious character reception is possible.

In 'Character and interformality' (CBR), he explores further the dichotomy of form and content in relation to the communication of the self, by making a distinction between two concepts: *self presentation and self representation*. He writes:

> Self-representation is the verbal act of describing the self and its world. It conveys a thought-content – our history, our personality, our tastes – and it is a form of self-disclosing communication especially popular in highly verbal cultures. [. . .]
> Self-presentation, from the linguistic point of view, conveys the self's being via the unconscious form of the narrative. It is the formal movement of one's self acting upon the object world.[4]

So when we think our thoughts and express them in words, we are intentionally *representing* to the other person elements of our self and our internal world. This will be related to the conscious internal narrative we have about ourself, but it will also involve a partly unconscious mix of, for example, clarity and obscurity, honesty and dissembling, depth and superficiality. At the same time, however, the other person will be receiving a deeper, non-verbal communication, a direct *presentation* of our character that is not crafted by our consciousness. Self presentation speaks through actions – physical movements and gestures, facial expressions and idiosyncratic forms of speech.

The transmission of mental content and the unconscious effects of idiom are two different and complementary categories of communication.

The person with whom we are talking will find it disturbing if there is too great a disparity between our self presentation and our self representation. This is rather like the double message deliberately created by a film-maker who uses incidental music that is at odds with the overt content of a scene. In this situation, we sense instinctively that it is the music – the non-verbal communication – that holds the greater truth. Because of its direct links with the unconscious, form is always more revealing than content.

Bollas suggests that in any interaction between two people, both are inevitably, though often in a subtle way, restructured internally by the encounter. He terms this process *interformality*: the reciprocal effects of the movement of the idiomatic forms of two selves. This process begins in advance of the actual event. Thinking about a forthcoming meeting with a friend awakens both conscious associative thoughts and unconscious interrelated constellations, as we anticipate the effect on us of this particular person.

He maintains that this process of interformality is, to a greater or lesser extent, inherently traumatic because it causes a rupture in the self state we were experiencing prior to the encounter. Whether the conscious effect on us is enjoyable or disturbing, we often find ourselves responding to this micro-trauma with a need to talk to someone about it. In doing this, we are translating the experience into a form that will render it thinkable, moving it from the presentational to the representational so that it can be mediated by consciousness. Bollas writes:

> Talking aims to transform the real into the symbolic, and even if this fails to represent the presentations of the experience it *adheres* to the experience and carries its after-effect in verbal form. Even if we do not turn to actual others we may have an internal dialogue about the recent encounter in which memory functions as a dynamic container for the after-effects of the real.[5]

He points out that this is one important function of the psychoanalytic situation. As the patient describes a social encounter, she is transforming its unconscious impact by making it containable in words and thoughts.

Inevitably, both self representation and self presentation play a part in the clinical relationship – and this works both ways. The analyst is attuned both to the patient's narrative and to the subtext presented by her character. In turn, although he responds to the patient at the level of representation, offering observations and interpretations, at the same time he too will be communicating at a more subtle level via the particular flavour of his choice of words and his vocal inflexions. The form of the analyst's response will communicate something about what he has perceived, operating unconsciously from, and within, the presentational realm of his own character. Analyst and patient are both in-formed by the impact of the other.

So how can we define our knowledge of character? Bollas writes:

> This is a knowledge that *just is*. Such knowledge is part of the matrix of human intuition. We intuit one another; as the other's medium, we have been in-formed of the other's idiom of being. And we use this information to guide us in the countless unconscious decisions about what to say, when to say it, how to say it, and all the subtle cues that we pass back to the other as part of the movement of interformality.[6]

Separating out the concepts of idiom, self and character – three distinct but intimately connected aspects of our subjectivity – helps us to clarify, and to think about, aspects of our internal experience. The clinical situation involves two idioms, two complex selves and the mutual unconscious impact of two people. Keeping this complexity in mind may help the clinician avoid reductive assumptions about the internal world of the patient. Using our awareness of the intricate byways of our own unique, forming intelligence, we hope to enable our patients to explore with greater creative freedom the complex patterns created by their innate idiom, their internal self relationships and the playing out of their character in the external world.

Notes

1 Bollas, C. 'Character and interformality', CBR p.240.
2 Ibid., p.242.
3 Bollas, C. 'Being a character', BC p.62.
4 Bollas, C. 'Character and interformality', CBR p.241.
5 Ibid., p.242.
6 Ibid., p.247.

Chapter 7

Evocative objects

Key papers

'The evocative object' (BC)
'The evocative object world' (EOW)
'The spirit of the object as the hand of fate' (SO)
'Perceptive identification' (FM)

Key concepts: *evocative objects; structural integrity; perceptive identification; projective, mnemic, aleatory and terminal objects; aesthetic dejection*

We shall now explore in detail another core aspect of Bollas's theory: the evocative effect of objects and the interplay between object and idiom. It is a theme that recurs throughout his work, perhaps more than any other, and he provides a chronological overview of the development of these ideas in the third chapter of *The Evocative Object World*.

The term 'British Object Relations School' originated in order to make a distinction between Freud's instinct-based model of the mind and the theories of Klein, Winnicott and the early Independents, all of whom regarded the infant's early relationship with objects as central to the formation and development of the psyche.

However, the term obscures a crucial difference. For Klein, the concept of object relations referred principally to internal, phantasy objects derived from instincts, and in particular from the struggle with the primitive anxieties (innate aggression and envy) associated with the death instinct. In contrast, Independent theorists, following Balint, Fairbairn and Winnicott, prioritised the infant's relationship with human objects in the external environment.

Bollas's exploration of the interaction between the self and the object world develops the Independent point of view, offering a rich vein of thinking about human subjectivity. His highly creative and detailed conceptual approach to the question of how and why we interact with external objects is innovative in three senses. First, his theory of the receptive unconscious proposes that perceptions of the object world are central to the formation and the functioning of the mind. Second, he deals extensively with our experience of the *inanimate* world – something unusual in psychoanalytic thinking. Third, he explores the idea that objects are significant, not merely because of what we project into them, but because of their own intrinsic qualities.

For Bollas, the selection and use of objects is a primary means of expressing and elaborating the idiom of the individual. As we saw in Chapter 2, his theory of the receptive unconscious involves a two-way process. The unconscious mind is constituted, not only from matrices of repressed traumatic experiences, as Freud maintained, but also from psychically significant elements of the object world that are invited into the unconscious for creative reasons. Each new impression becomes part of a network of evolving psychic genera – matrices of unconscious thinking. As well as forming ever more intricate interconnections within the mind, these also generate a search for related objects that will further articulate the self's idiom. An object will be evocative if it has unconscious resonance for that individual.

In Chapter 3 we explored the idea of the mother as a transformational object, instinctively providing her baby with experiences that are in tune with his idiom and that may therefore bring about a transformation of his self state – what Bollas terms an *aesthetic moment*. As young children develop, they encounter an increasingly diverse object world and they develop correspondingly differentiated ways of responding to it. In their play, they will unconsciously choose a specific toy in order to perform a particular type of thinking. Their use of the object is an extension of their internal reality.

As adults, too, we are constantly making choices in our interaction with the world around us. Although many of these decisions are made at a conscious level, they are also imbued with unconscious resonance. In the morning we choose which clothes to wear, but if we are not well in tune with ourselves that day we may get it wrong and feel uncomfortable – rather like the mother who offers the baby the wrong toy at the wrong moment. This commonplace example demonstrates the close link between unconscious self states and the selection of external objects. Other choices are made more fleetingly – we automatically choose a mug for our coffee, we glance at certain shop windows and not others.

Bollas points out that psychoanalytic writing has rarely considered the world of inanimate objects, yet this is a crucial aspect of our relationship with external reality. In fact, he makes a radical claim:

> For the unconscious there is no difference between a material and a non-material evocative object; both are equally capable of putting the self through a complex inner experience.[1]

In other words, just as we are subtly restructured internally by an encounter with another human being, each aspect of the inanimate environment will also have a direct presentational effect on us.

We may use an object for projective purposes, either to contain a part of our self that we wish to be rid of, or for safekeeping. However, there is another aspect to our use of objects, and this concerns the interaction of our idiom with the object's own intrinsic characteristics – something that we receive from the object. Bollas writes that we are affected by the *structural integrity* of the thing-in-itself. These two aspects of object relating – the projective and the receptive – will usually occur simultaneously.

Let us imagine two different experiences of attending a meeting. On the first occasion we meet in a bare, modern room, painted white, with a low ceiling and strip lighting. The second meeting is held in an Elizabethan wood-panelled library, in which shelves of leather-bound volumes are interspersed with ancestral portraits.

The experience of entering these two rooms is radically different on many levels. We respond unconsciously with our individual associations and projections, but irrespective of what we contribute from our internal world, we are also powerfully affected, both consciously and unconsciously, by what the two rooms present us with. Each has its own idiom; each will in-form us in a particular way, and the two very different experiences will stay with us after the meetings are over.

In the third chapter of *The Freudian Moment*, Bollas posits a developmental stage, following the Kleinian depressive position and Winnicott's stage of transitional object use, when the child becomes aware of the integrity of the object. Bollas terms this *perceptive identification*. Winnicott's transitional object is significant because it stands for other experiences, but in the stage of perceptive identification it is the specificity of the object itself that is crucial. It involves the recognition that the object has an existence distinct from the self, and that the self is affected by contact with it. Bollas writes: 'This model presupposes the *jouissance* of difference (not similarity) and implicitly appreciates the separateness of the object.'[2]

He points out that the capacity for perceptive identification is a prerequisite for the mature form of love. Rather than being governed by narcissistic processes, it represents a true depth of intimacy with the object, which is loved for its own sake and not because it reflects the self. Here he contrasts this concept with projective identification:

> If projective identification gets inside the other, perceptive identification stands outside to perceive the other. The term 'identification' means quite different things for each concept. In projective identification it means identifying with the object, in perceptive identification it means perceiving the identity of the object. Both forms of knowing need to work in tandem with one another in a creative oscillation between appreciating the integrity of the object and perceiving its identity, and then projecting parts of the self into the object, a form of imagination.[3]

In 'The evocative object' (BC), Bollas discusses in detail many aspects of the self's interaction with the external world, developing the idea that we seek and select specific objects because they offer distinct *forms* of experience. They represent 'concepts of being' to which our idiom is attracted. He writes:

> objects suggest psychologically distinct types of self experience, so that when a person employs an object it is of interest to note what is conceptually solicited. Mountain climbing, chamber music playing, snorkelling, and partygoing are different experiences involving different objects and therefore different concepts of one's being that ideationalize psychologically different forms for being, use, and relating. So as we think of engaging with each of these objects, a different psychic notion of what we shall be doing comes to mind, which operates on conscious, preconscious and unconscious levels.[4]

We relate to objects in many different ways. We experience them through *physical* sensations; we are affected *structurally* by their individual integrity, and *conceptually*, as different objects elicit in us specific trains of thought. Objects can also function *symbolically*, as we associate their names with other signifiers; *mnemically*, as we endow them with personal historical significance; and *projectively*, as we use them to process aspects of our internal world. Different objects therefore fulfil different functions for the self.

Bollas explores in detail the intrapsychic effects of the various categories of object, and we shall consider three of these.

The *mnemic object* relates to memory. It is a form of subjective object that contains a fragment of self experience from the past and allows it to be re-contacted in the present. Whereas projective identification generally results in the loss of the projected part of the self, mnemic objects keep us in touch with former self states, and they can therefore hold a particular evocative richness. As an example, Bollas cites Proust's madeleine, which functions not merely as a vessel to contain a particular memory but as a portal to a vast realm of proliferating associations. These highly cathected objects create islands of intensity and significance in the unconscious, leaving an imprint that combines the qualities of the object-in-itself with its individual meaning for us – its interaction with our idiom and our history.

So we are drawn to some objects for the evocative potential of their structural integrity to resonate with our idiom, and we unconsciously designate others as receptacles for fragments of our experience. However, we also frequently encounter phenomena that arrive unexpectedly. These Bollas terms *aleatory objects* – objects that arrive by chance. He writes:

> these aleatory objects evoke psychic textures which do not reflect the valorisations of desire. We have not, as it were, selected the aleatory object to express an idiom of self. Instead, we are played upon by the inspiring arrival of the unselected, which often yields a very special type of pleasure – that of surprise. It opens us up, liberating an area like a key fitting a lock.[5]

We may seek the desired, but we are also enlivened by the spontaneous activities of our objects. Surprise is a very particular experience. It breaches our defences; we are flooded with condensed associations, both conscious and unconscious, and this often produces a transformation, a sense of inner expansion. However, we are able to relish surprise only if we can cope with the disruption it causes to our internal world.

Unlike mnemic and aleatory objects, *terminal objects* are not evocative and they do not sponsor the elaboration of the self's idiom. They relate to being-states that became encapsulated in early life because they could not be conceptualised or symbolically represented. Terminal objects therefore embody primitive states of defence and withdrawal.

In the clinical situation, a patient who is governed by a terminal object will be cut off, both from her own unconscious creativity and from the desire for connection with external life. She will have a profound resistance to associative thinking and to any elaboration of the self. In terms of Bollas's model of the unconscious, these are people dominated by matrices of trauma, out of touch with the creative activity of psychic genera, and this situation typically produces a powerful countertransference reaction in the analyst. He senses his own associative thinking shutting down in the face of the patient's addiction to the deadening power of the terminal object.

Bollas regards object selection as a form of unconscious thinking. We choose an object that meets some internal need in that moment. Its intrinsic qualities resonate with us idiosyncratically and evoke aspects of our idiom, our instinctive sense of form. In this way, external reality meets internal reality. In 'Aspects of self experiencing' (BC), he writes:

> As we constantly endow objects with psychic meaning, we therefore walk amidst our own significance, and, sometimes long after we have invested a thing, we encounter it again, releasing its meaning, although, as I shall maintain, such signifieds do not often reach consciousness.[6]

When we find ourselves in a complex environment made up of many different objects, each individual aspect of what we perceive, both consciously and unconsciously, will elicit in us a different self state. Bollas illustrates the multi-layered character of this experience with the example of entering a large department store:

> Each section of the store, each part of the section, each unit of visual space, contains evocative objects. As we see them their design elicits feelings within us, their function comes to mind, their names – generic and brand – come up in consciousness. As to the unconscious registration of such objects, we can only assume that just as the store clusters like-objects in such units, our mind does much the same thing, with the salient exception that we add personal meaning to each and every one of the things we see.[7]

So as we move through the array of experiences offered by the external world, the objects act on us in different ways and we react with many specific forms of response. Each of these will be governed by our own particular aesthetic intelligence, and each will spark its own web of associations. There will also be a spectrum of internal intensity that involves the polarities of familiarity versus novelty. Some people crave new experiences; others gravitate to the known. Our object choices reflect our predisposition towards the degree of stimulation that resonates most comfortably with our idiom.

In *China on the Mind*, Bollas discusses the object relating that takes place through the medium of poems, and in particular the pared-down, highly evocative forms of poetry that are traditional in the East. Here projection into objects is refined into a subtle art form, as intense personal feelings are contained and represented by individual elements of the natural world.

This process is embodied in the structure of the Chinese language. A single written character consists of a pictorial cluster of associated ideas that combine to convey inherently complex meanings that will speak to each person differently. It brings apparently disparate objects into a resonant relationship:

> The free-standing nature of each image, the surprising juxtaposition of objects, is a thing unto itself that has an evocative integrity. [. . .]
> These poems inherit and use the ideographic nature of the Chinese language; each character is itself a small poem. They unite image and sound with personal emotion and yet weave the particular into the social order. A brief poem can thus be both unique and universal at the same time.[8]

In 'Architecture and the unconscious' (EOW), an essay written originally for an audience of architects, Bollas explores the impact of buildings as evocative objects that both reflect our individual unconscious thinking and provide a metaphor for aspects of the mind. Although this paper is not couched in psychoanalytic language, it includes implicit references to the dichotomies of destiny and fate, and of psychic trauma and psychic genera.

Bollas suggests that a new building can offer a creative vision of the future, but it can also impinge on us as an invasion of the present *by* the future. Its design will involve a combination of functionality and evocative intention. If it replaces a previous building, it will be an object that symbolises both creation and obliteration. It can therefore represent birth, but also the presence of death and liberation from previous attachments.

Just as every individual building has its idiomatic presence and will be responded to as a unique object, Bollas suggests that each city also has its own idiom that creates a characteristic evocative effect. He points out that even in our own familiar environment we are likely to be unaware of the function of many of the buildings. Without conceptual referrants, they affect us as purely visual objects via their idiomatic form. They therefore remain in the order of perception and imagination; the preconceptual maternal order.

As with all objects, our experience of the built environment is a combination of our projections and associations and the effect on us of its structural integrity. As a city transforms over time, new architectural forms – appearing first as aleatory objects – will introduce us to new perceptions. A building that has played a significant part in our life will also function as a mnemic object, a gateway to past experiences and to all the memories and associations that accompany them. The city, as an evocative object, is a complex unconscious process.

Bollas's exploration of the interweaving of internal and the external realities provides a perspective from which to consider various forms of pathology, and the patient's attitude to the object world can be an important diagnostic criterion. Energy and alacrity in the selection of objects serve the innate drive to elaborate idiom, and freedom in the interaction with a wide range of objects is one indicator of psychic health.

However, new objects, especially those that invite a passionate, instinctive engagement, can rock the boat. In people who are governed by matrices of trauma, the instinct to search for generative experiences becomes limited by the need to protect the self. Trauma restricts genera. Using Winnicott's concept of the 'intermediate area',[9] Bollas writes:

> Some individuals are reluctant to live in the third area (the intermediate area of experience), insisting that the invitational feature of the object be declined. They impose their view on the object world and blunt the evocative – transformational – facet of objects in the field. They may narrow the choice of objects, eliminating those with a high evocative potential.[10]

In Chapter 5 we looked at Bollas's concept of normotic pathology, when people live a life governed by conforming to social norms at the expense of investment in the internal, subjective world. Although organised external activities may be engaged in with enthusiasm (this is the ideal team player), the normotic's object choices will not reflect exploratory freedom. Freud's repression of the primitive, Winnicott's false self, the frustration inherent in rigid conventionality: all of these can mititate against the elaboration of idiom. The spontaneous gesture is mistrusted, and engagement with the object world is used in the service, not of individual expression, but of belonging at all costs.

In 'Preoccupation unto death' (CU), Bollas discusses three related self states that are essentially object related: concentration, preoccupation and obsession. They represent a spectrum, from intense creative engagement at one end to intractable psychopathology at the other. Here he differentiates between obsession and preoccupation:

> Pathological obsession is aimed at maintaining a terminal object that *ends* all unconscious use of the object: ideational, affective, somatic, or transferential. A preoccupation allows for the migration of feelings into the situation: the object is subjected to use in that it is subjected to fantasy and can therefore elaborate aspects of the subject.[11]

> The obsessed person feels impinged upon by the object; as in its ancient usage, it is like being taken over by a demon, driven crazy by an intrusive idea. The preoccupied person seems to do something rather different: he conjures a mental space into which he brings all of his interests – in this case one object – to the exclusion of all else.[12]

Sometimes, whether in a close personal relationship or a work situation, or in the feelings we have about living in a particular place, we can find ourselves caught in a fundamental mismatch between self and object. Bollas suggests that some objects will never resonate with us, and this can be a matter not of pathology but of idiom: we simply find certain things alien. If this situation is not resolvable, it can produce a profound form of depression that he terms *aesthetic dejection.*[13]

One result of psychoanalytic treatment can be an alteration in the patient's habitual approach to objects. As the internal world becomes a less dangerous place, she will gradually give up the defensive use of elements in the environment – to maintain a pathological status quo, for example, or to shut down thinking – and develop a new capacity for the spontaneous and creative use of a wider variety of objects.

Much psychoanalytic thinking is weighted in favour of internal reality and the role of unconscious phantasy, but Bollas frequently emphasises, in addition, the importance of lived experience in the external world. Patients new to psychoanalysis often equate the concept of the unconscious with the conscious *feeling* of things being deeply meaningful. If they continue to regard insular subjectivity as the arena for psychoanalytic work, there is a danger that they may leave their everyday lives outside the consulting room. Bollas believes that, on the contrary, in order for patients to become more in touch with their idiomatic core they need to develop an interest, not only in the profound themes and dilemmas that have brought them into analysis, but also in the minutiae of their ordinary life, as it is these details that reveal the unconscious thinking represented by their object choices.

In 'The evocative object' (BC), he writes:

> the work that characterises the unconscious ego is the nonrepresentational unconscious that selects and uses objects in order to disseminate the self into experiencings that articulate and enrich it.[14]

Notes

1 Bollas, C. 'The evocative object world', EOW p.79.
2 Bollas, C. 'Perceptive identification', FM p.66.
3 Ibid., p.68.
4 Bollas, C. 'The evocative object', BC p.34.
5 Ibid., p.37.
6 Bollas, C. 'Aspects of self experiencing', BC pp.12–13.
7 Bollas, C. 'The evocative object world', EOW p.80.
8 Bollas, C. *China on the Mind*, p.37.
9 Winnicott, D. (1971) 'The place where we live'. In *Playing and Reality*. London: Tavistock.
10 Bollas, C. 'Aspects of self experiencing', BC p.31.
11 Bollas, C. 'Preoccupation unto death', CU pp.78–9 (original italics).
12 Ibid., p.79.
13 Bollas, C. 'The evocative object world', EOW pp.90–2.
14 Ibid., p.42.

Chapter 8

Unconscious complexity

Key papers

'Dissemination' (CU)
'Articulations of the unconscious' (FM)
'Psychic transformations' (FM)
The Infinite Question

Key concepts: *categories of communication; ramifying lines of thought; psychic focus and psychic dissemination; radical free associations*

Having examined the interrelation between the internal world and the world of external objects, we shall now look in more detail at the nature of the unconscious that is suggested by Bollas's metapsychology.

The model of the receptive unconscious proposes a mind that is astonishingly intricate. Bollas employs a musical analogy as a way of conceptualising this complexity. He suggests that the elements present in a psychoanalytic session can be pictured visually like an orchestral score, in which there is both a horizontal progression from left to right, representing temporal movement, and a vertical axis consisting of an individual line for each instrument. These play simultaneously within the musical work with varying degrees of prominence, conflict and co-operation.

In this analogy, the instrumental lines represent the many threads of meaning, both conscious and unconscious, that play a part in the session. They will be expressed in many different forms, and Bollas describes these as *categories of communication*. They might include, for example: the patient's conscious narrative and its presentation; thoughts and feelings as they evolve in both patient and analyst; body expression; the diverse strands of the patient's individual history and the shared history of the analytic work; the predominant transference relationship and other transient transferential phenomena; the wider relational implications of the narrative; fluctuating intrapsychic modes (for example, paranoid-schizoid or depressive); the projective use of the analytic object; the patient's enactments of aspects of her character; periodicities of moods and psychic intensities; the uses of humour, both defensive and spontaneous; and unconscious psychic structures that represent paradigms derived from her early experience (the unthought known).

Many more items could be added to this list, and the complexity does not stop there. If we put any individual category under the microscope, we find it branching out, like fractals, creating a potentially infinite network. Each one could be examined and deconstructed, but as an example, let us take the category of language.

Alongside the manifest intended meaning of the patient's narrative, the linguistic category will also include grammar and syntax – the pre-existing rules governing the particular language that is being spoken – and the idiomatic version of the language characteristic of that patient. This will include, for example, a unique combination of restriction and expressiveness; an idiosyncratic approach to narrative logic, description and figures of speech; the timbre or tonal quality of her voice and its degree of appropriateness to the subject matter, in both its conscious and unconscious aspects; the volume of her speech, habitual inflexions, rhythmic variations and changes in tempo; and the proportion, length and quality of silences.

All these linguistic elements operate together to create a ramifying network of conscious and unconscious communication. In *The Infinite Question*, Bollas writes:

> words evoke clusters of ideas that will link with other clusters, themselves also moving along in sequence. So we see that even within the linguistic category alone – and if we focus just on the phonemic and semantic capability of words – we already have a thicket of meanings moving along in sequential time. If we add dimensions from the sonic category – stress, pitch, cadence, duration, silence – these lines of expression open up the field of unconscious expression even more widely, thickly and deeply.[1]

He draws our attention to the subtle, fleeting micro-communications that accompany the content of the patient's narrative. For example, thematic emphasis might be conveyed by a sudden hesitation, a change in volume, or a repetition. A word that keeps recurring is often a complex signifier, representing various meanings that may relate to different lines of unconscious thinking. A moment of syntactical confusion might indicate a quick, subliminal reliving of a past micro-trauma that deferred affect and understanding.

Sometimes a patient will produce a non sequitur, a comment apparently unconnected with previous material. Bollas terms this a *radical free association*. It creates a striking moment, often resulting in an intensification of unconscious perception in the analyst. Numerous changes of tack indicate psychic fluidity and a freedom in making unconscious connections. Similarly, the appearance of new metaphors or a particular vividness in the choice of words produces a deepening of communication.

There may be a change in the form of the patient's presentation as she opens herself up to a different category of communication. She may, for example, move from the narrative to the projective in order to facilitate further unconscious ideas. Sometimes a period of quiet reflectiveness is ruptured by an outburst of something theatrical or childlike; a breaking down of adult syntax might indicate the presence of an infantile part of the self. At a certain moment the patient may seem to be expressing herself in the voice of another person, often her mother or father. This unconscious articulation of an identification involves a convergence of the relational and sonic categories.

When different orders of articulation are used simultaneously to express the same idea, this produces a particular intensity of unconscious focus. At other times, different lines of unconscious thought may be present simultaneously. The narration of an everyday event may be what is uppermost in the mind of the patient, but the analyst may be struck by, for example, a lack of fit between her words and what is communicated through the body. She may be speaking from within the transference, but at the same time she may be articulating quite different unconscious preoccupations through the form of her narrative sequence or the sonic effects of her voice, which can either underline or contradict the conscious meaning of the narrative.

It will be clear that Bollas does not generally share the view that a breakdown in psychic cohesion constitutes an attack on the analyst's mind. He maintains that the spontaneous juxtaposition of apparently unconnected ideas, far from indicating an avoidance of meaning, is evidence of a deep level of unconscious communication. Certain forms of expression may indicate defensiveness: the patient who is persistently glib or flippant, skating quickly between superficial objects without landing anywhere long enough to think, may be avoiding analytic engagement. However, what might appear manic – pressured speech, brevity, urgency – can also represent a flooding of unconscious contents.

The ramifying potential of each category of communication means that many unconscious themes will inevitably be present in any one moment. At certain points some of these threads, like some of the orchestral instruments, may be silent for a while, but this does not mean that their influence disappears. When the analyst chooses to make an interpretation this will highlight a certain aspect, but it will always involve leaving many others out. As long as it remains relatively uninterfered with, this intricate, interwoven orchestration will give shape to the session, led by the patient's unconscious.

Certain categories will tend to be especially congruent with the idiom of any individual, and the various forms of communication require different sorts of engagement from the analyst. With one person he might frequently find himself responding to what is expressed through tone of voice, whereas another patient might communicate non-verbally through various parts of the body as she lies on the couch. No two patients give the analyst the same experience, and each clinician will inevitably respond most naturally to certain forms of communication. Although awareness is expanded through analytic training, the analyst can never escape the predispositions of his own idiom. This is one way to conceptualise the issue of 'fit' between clinician and patient.

Bollas's highly complex view of the unconscious develops out of Freud's concept of 'nodal points': points of psychic intensity formed by the convergence of unconscious threads. In the following passage from *The Interpretation of Dreams*, Freud describes the mechanism whereby the various meanings of significant moments from the dream day are condensed into a hypercathected dream image:

> [dream thoughts] usually emerge as a complex of thoughts and memories of the most intricate possible structure, with all the attributes of the trains of thought familiar to us in waking life. They are not infrequently trains of thought starting out from more than one centre, though having points of contact.[2]

Bollas emphasises that this process is not restricted to dreams. At any single moment during the day we are operating on many overlapping planes of psychic reality, with moments of intensity continually engendered as our internal mental activity encounters evocative objects in the external world. It is these hyperinvested moments that create psychic genera. In 'Psychic transformations' (FM), he describes the texture of the unconscious:

> Our unconscious is a dynamic factory of thought that knits together "infinite" lines of thought that combine and grow. Some of the lines

come together for a while and create nodal points, and because of that increased psychic weight may come into consciousness, but all along, of course, there are thousands and thousands of other lines of thought in this ramifying factory that continue separately. [. . .]

This infinite combination of growing thought is, in my view, Freud's core theory of the unconscious and clearly a model of mental development.[3]

This process of intensification and ramification also manifests as a duality in our subjective experience. In 'Dissemination' (CU), Bollas describes how, moment-to-moment, we oscillate between psychic focus and a state of diffuseness.

To take an everyday example: we are walking down the street in a state of reverie. Suddenly something catches our eye and we have an experience of psychic intensity. The object 'holds our attention' – it contains our subjectivity – and we then find ourself fragmenting into a web of associated thoughts, memories and feelings. Then we walk on. As the object leaves our sight it also gradually leaves our mind; the associations dissolve from our consciousness and we return to a diffuse, dreamy state until another object claims our attention. The more profound the intensity of the moment, the more it will disseminate into divergent constituent thoughts. Bollas writes:

as we think of people or places or events they are always linked to a group of ideas (whether we recall them or not) and it is this movement of the groups of ideas, or matrices of thought, that I believe best characterizes how we think.[4]

This model proposes a level of creativity in the unconscious that faces the psychoanalyst with almost bewildering complexity. When an analyst gives an account of a session to colleagues, infinitely more will be left out than will be reported, and some categories of communication are easier to convey to a third party than others. It is impossible to capture adequately in words a subtle shift in atmosphere or the nuances of a person's tone of voice. Inevitably, the totality of the experience will be simplified and to some extent misrepresented, and what one analyst chooses to take up with the patient may not be what appears to another afterwards as the most prevalent issue.

However tempting it may be in such clinical discussions to try to pin down exactly what is going on, it will be impossible for the analyst to follow consciously more than a few of the lines of thought that are present.

It may be humbling to realise how much we miss, but it can be salutary if it helps steer us away from reductionism and oversimplification in our understanding of what is happening in a session.

It may be that the patient is wedded to a simplistic version of herself, leaving the analyst to hold an awareness of the deeper aspects of her internal world. When such patients begin to encounter their psychic complexity – faced, perhaps, with a moment of paradoxical thinking or contradiction – they sometimes feel they must be lying. They have a need to limit themselves to a single meaning because without this certainty they risk a sense of disintegration. In this situation it often comes as a relief to find that contradictions can be sanctioned and even welcomed by the analyst who, far from pinning the patient down to what is 'true', transforms a fear into a sense of creative possibility. Bollas writes: 'The technique practised by a psychoanalyst implicitly recognizes the dense, moving complexity that is the patient's fragmenting elaboration of idiom.'[5]

We might assume psychic health to be a relatively simple state that becomes complicated by pathology. However, Bollas proposes the opposite: that symptoms produce restriction and simplified functioning, whereas health implies a capacity for ever-expanding intrapsychic experience. He warns psychoanalytic clinicians against limiting themselves to a concern with pathology; he regards the creative potential of unconscious complexity as a more fundamental aspect of the mind than symptoms, repression, resistances or transferences. He writes:

> If I had to pick one area in which I think psychoanalysis suffers from a devastating blindness it is here, in the failure to comprehend the unconscious creativity of the analysand.[6]

Notes

1 Bollas, C. *The Infinite Question*, p.27.
2 Freud, S. (1900) 'The interpretation of dreams', *The Complete Psychological Works of Sigmund Freud*, ed. Strachey, J. *(London: Hogarth) IV*, pp.310–11.
3 Bollas, C. 'Psychic transformations', FM p.17.
4 Ibid., p.29.
5 Bollas, C. 'A separate sense', CU p.40.
6 Bollas, C. 'Articulations of the unconscious', FM p.54.

Chapter 9

Free association

Key papers

'Free association' (EOW)
'The goals of psychoanalysis?' (MT)
'Creativity and psychoanalysis' (MT)
The Infinite Question

Key concepts: *phonemic links; polysemous words; language transformers; logic of sequence; chains of question and answer*

With this model of unconscious complexity in mind, we turn now to
what is probably Bollas's most extensive contribution to the theory of
clinical technique: his development of the concept of free association.
He describes Freud's fundamental clinical innovation as 'the most revolutionary accomplishment of psychoanalysis'.[1]

Although the use of free association has always been a prominent
feature, both of his own clinical approach and of his explorations with
colleagues, over the past 15 years his advocacy of this has become a
passionate campaign. With his monograph titled *Free Association* (first
published in 2002 by Icon Books and reprinted as the first chapter of
The Evocative Object World), and subsequently with *The Infinite Question*, he offers a comprehensive exploration of the theory and practice
of Freud's psychoanalytic technique. Although in his clinical work he
will also make full use of many other aspects of theory and practice, he
regards free association as the central tool at all points in an analysis and
in all pathologies, from neurosis to schizophrenia.

It is not possible to include all the elements of his discussion of this
topic, and detailed technical aspects will not be addressed here. His way of
working comes across in clinical vignettes throughout his writings, but his
most extensive technical discussion is to be found in *The Infinite Question*.

Whilst acknowledging that the British focus on the transference relationship has yielded invaluable understandings, Bollas points out that
it has also brought about a change of emphasis, and with it a radical
sidelining of Freud's principal route to understanding the unconscious.
Free association has come to be taken for granted, and today, certainly
in the UK, it produces little curiosity or exploration and it is generally
addressed very minimally in clinical trainings. It has become an assumption whose importance has dwindled.

However, if it has become marginalised in modern practice, Bollas
suggests that this is due in part to the many revisions that took place
in Freud's own work. From the beginning, the psychoanalytic focus
continually shifted: from the uncovering of repressed ideas and latent
instinctual wishes, to the removal of resistances, then to liberation of the
libido from its fixations and the freeing of the ego. These various aims all
represent different desires in the analyst, and as Freud's developing fields
of interest brought new goals, he became more interested in what was
produced by free association than in the efficacy of the method in itself.
Content took over from form, deflecting attention away from the deep
complexity of mental life towards specific manifestations of pathology.

If we accept that free association provides access to unconscious contents, then our understanding of this concept must depend on our model of
the unconscious mind. For example, if we are thinking from the point of
view of Freud's repression model, we shall expect the patient's associations
to reveal clues to censored, ego-dystonic material. On the other hand, if the
analyst's mind is focused on the transference as the central unconscious
issue, he will be on the lookout for evidence of this in the patient's narrative.

So what are the implications for this technique of Bollas's theory of
the receptive unconscious?

In proposing a psyche constituted of a continuously evolving web of
associated ideas, he greatly expands the scope of the concept of free
association. As Freud pointed out, it is not just our dream images that are
saturated with condensations of related thoughts; in our waking lives,
too, we think associatively. In the clinical situation, free association
(which Bollas sometimes refers to as *free talking*) is first and foremost a
means of gaining access to the threads of this complex internal network,
as previously unthought ideas find their way to consciousness through
the narrated details of everyday life.

Bollas is committed to refocusing our attention on Freud's original
and profound discovery as the foundation for psychoanalytic practice,
and he begins his exploration by reminding the reader of the basics.
With the analyst in a state of 'evenly hovering attention',[2] the patient is

encouraged to speak her private, inner monologue, which is thus brought into a dialogue as part of a unique two-person relationship. He emphasises that Freud gives particular weight, not to disagreeable thoughts that are obviously dynamically repressed, but to those that seem trivial or irrelevant. If the patient simply voices what she can of her ever-present private narrative, links will emerge that bring unexpected fragments of the unconscious to the surface.

The idea is radical: the patient must discard the quest to know in favour of simply reporting what is there at that moment in her conscious mind. Contrary to the expectations of many people embarking on psychoanalytic treatment, the process does not depend on the patient forcing herself to recount her most disturbing hidden thoughts. Like Freud, Bollas asks the new patient simply to speak about whatever is crossing her mind. However, he emphasises the need to be specific. The tendency to generalise or to offer 'headlines' shuts down the unconscious participation of both analyst and patient. It is through immersion in *detail*, however apparently insignificant, that the unconscious speaks.

In this context, what do we mean by the word 'free'? We can never be free from unconscious censorship – indeed, as Freud showed, the free associative process inevitably reveals unconscious conflicts, and these are a valuable aspect of the patient's communication. But other freedoms are crucial: the freedom not to plan the contents of the session, so that the logic of unconscious thinking can reveal itself; the free movement between subjects; the freedom to interrupt a line of thought without explanation if other thoughts break in. There is also freedom from the conventions of ordinary relational language, and from the social requirement of considering the other person's needs.

And, most centrally, there is the freedom not to make sense. We do not require patients to present themselves in a consistent or intelligible fashion. Bollas acknowledges that they might experience some initial anxiety about this unusual activity: 'yet in time they may come to appreciate this remarkable and strange freedom to speak in fragments, each telling a small cameo of a different order of thought.'[3]

Implicitly bringing together Freud's two concepts, *freie Assoziation* (the linking of ideas) and *freier Einfall* (the dropping into consciousness of an unexpected thought), he describes the free associative process as follows:

> talking about what is on the mind, moving from one topic to another in a freely moving sequence that does not follow an agenda. The analyst may encourage the patient to speak those thoughts at the

back of the mind and, like Freud, will emphasise the need to interrupt a narrative if *other* thoughts arise; but even if patients rarely
achieve this completely, they are nevertheless free associating if
they move freely from one topic to the next in an hour.[4]

Free association reflects, in various ways, all the dualities that we have
encountered in Bollas's thinking. The maternal and the paternal drive
opposite forms of desire: the expansive articulation that gives form to
our idiom, versus the focused epistemophilic instinct – the drive to know.
In view of Freud's conscious wish for mechanistic, scientific certainties,
his invention of free association was a rather striking unconscious move.
Bollas writes: 'in requesting this kind of talk Freud released us all to be
continuously mysterious to ourselves and others.'[5]

He suggests that the free associative technique fundamentally subverts
the patriarchal Western order that privileges consciousness and objective
thinking. When the analyst opens up the patient's narrative by asking for
associations to a word or an idea, the paternal structure of the conscious
mind is challenged. The psychoanalytic setting in itself bears the hall-
marks of the maternal – the patient reclines, submitting to the analyst's
care, in an atmosphere imbued with unconscious communication. Here,
Bollas links the clinical relationship to the maternal dyad:

> The analyst, in a state of even suspension – unintrusive, concentrat-
> ing, receptive, dreamy – derives this presentational craft from the
> constituents of maternal creativity. And just as the mother receives
> and transforms her infant's communications, conveying through
> each moment of maternal care a type of devotion to the develop-
> ment of the infant's idiom, so the psychoanalyst's function within
> the maternal order effectively elicits the analysand's presentation of
> idiom for further articulation.[6]

Free association involves a form of splitting. However, this is not the defensive splitting described by Klein, which is a prelude to projection, ridding
the self of unwanted contents. This is a splitting into innumerable associated
threads of meaning, and it is a way of making contact with unconsciously
related parts of the mind. If this breaking up of meaning cannot take place –
in cases of extreme obsessionality, for example, or severe depression –
consciousness becomes stuck instead of fluid. Bollas writes:

> Free association is creative destruction [. . .] It is essential to
> one's personal freedom to break up lucid unities of thought, lest

consciousness become a form of ideational incarceration. Indeed, the more profound a psychic intensity, the less permanent its registration in consciousness, for the ideas deriving immediately from it soon give birth to a plenitude of further and divergent thoughts which disseminate in countless ways.[7]

Within this fluctuating balance – maternal/paternal, focus/dissemination – the free associating patient presents the analyst with glimpses of latent thoughts. If the narrative is allowed to progress naturally, unconscious links will be made, and eventually themes will arrive in the consciousness in a thinkable form. In other words, if the unconscious is not interfered with, it will use the analytic situation for articulation, exploration and comprehension.

Bollas's theory of an infinitely complex unconscious is, as we have seen, very different from Freud's simple repression model. However, by focusing on the multiple coexisting aspects of the patient's internal world, he shifts the perspective of free association to bring it in line with Freud's conception of the sophisticated unconscious that creates the dream. He writes:

> Freud's theory of the density of unconscious processes, embedded in his theory of intersecting lines of thought, means that no one session could ever be focused on the retrieval of one or more particular repressed ideas. There will be points of convergence, and at times these will bring the discovery of forgotten material that may elucidate the structure of a symptom or help to unravel the meaning of a dream.[8]

Interlaced with all these complexities is the patient's relationship, in every area of his life, with evocative objects. Bollas's exploration of our encounter with the external world (discussed in Chapter 7) deepens our appreciation of the resonances in the patient's narrative and enhances our perception of the expression of idiom. He writes:

> Through free associating the patient unconsciously selects objects of desire and articulates, through these objects, evolving self experiences. [. . .] We're talking here, of course, of mental objects: of objects that come into mind through which nascent self-states are released into articulation.[9]

We shall now consider in more detail four aspects of free association that Bollas considers to be at its heart: the phonemic significance of words;

the logic of the unconscious sequence that governs the patient's narrative; the presence of an underlying process of question and answer; and the intrinsic therapeutic value of the free associative process.

Bollas's interest in the phonemic aspect of free association reflects his interest in French psychoanalysis. In 'Dissemination' (CU), he takes up Lacan's idea that an individual word can becomes a complex signifier by virtue of its sonic structure:

> Lacan's theory of the signifier indicates a logic operating through the structure of language [. . .] his understanding of the symbolic allows us to appreciate the thousands of separate logical evolutions that burst from a single event, each within its own logical chain.[10]

Although the patient might choose a certain word for a consciously intended meaning, the analyst may find himself struck by something in the *sound* of the word that suggests quite different unconscious links. Some words are polysemous; their individual syllables provide roots for further associations, introducing new clusters of ideas that will in turn produce their own chains of psychic significance. Like an overdetermined dream image, multiple meanings can therefore be condensed into a single evocative word. Bollas regards the choice of such language by the patient as an unconsciously creative activity. Often registered subliminally by the analyst, phonemic links are one of the ways in which the unconscious minds of patient and analyst communicate directly without involving consciousness.

Devices such as puns, rhyming, repetition and metaphor all indicate the presence of latent content and an unconscious desire to communicate. However, words can also be used to keep the other out, and patients who are rigidly defended against allowing contact with the internal world will tend to avoid using such resonant forms of language. In 'Normotic illness' (SO), Bollas coins the term *language transformers*.[11] These are clichéd phrases – 'You know what I mean'; 'It's really weird'; 'It's my worst nightmare' – that may be used casually and habitually by the patient as an unconscious means of denuding speech of evocative, idiomatic meaning and blocking communication.

It will be clear from the discussion of unconscious complexity in Chapter 8 that at any given moment in the session many distinct forms of logic are present and active. There is the logic of projection, in which the analysis becomes a theatre of multiple selves and multiple objects. There is the logic of transference and countertransference, in which elements of former relationships are unconsciously re-enacted. There is also the logic presented by manifestations of character structure. For Bollas, however, the core constituent in the free associative process is what Freud terms the *logic of sequence*.[12]

This refers to the unconscious, latent meaning contained in the sequence of apparently unconnected topics that appear in the course of a session. The crucial point here is that meaning lies not just in the manifest and latent content of what is said, but in *the unconscious thought that links one set of ideas to the next*. Bollas considers this to be a more significant form of unconscious representation than the occasional glimpses of repressed material provided by the patient's slips and unintended meanings, as it gives access to the vast network of associations that makes up the receptive unconscious. In *The Infinite Question*, he uses extended clinical examples in order to trace the unconscious logic revealed as the patient's material unfolds.

This sequential aspect of the analytic narrative is analogous to the inherent logic in a piece of music. Objectively, music takes place in time, and the listener's subjective experience is also of a temporal unfolding. It would make no sense to explore, or to attempt to understand, a musical work other than in the sequence in which it is written and heard. The early utterances of a patient in a session are rather like the opening harmonic moments in a piece of music or the first few notes of a melody: we can hope to interpret them only once they have acquired meaning within a context, once the logical sequence has been established.

Whenever the analyst intervenes in the narrative, the patient will have a response to the analyst's interpretations, and this is liable to disrupt the previous trajectory of the unconscious sequence. However, Bollas points out that a technique based on free association answers, at least in part, the accusation that psychoanalysis is lacking in objectivity. He writes: 'The order of the presentation of thoughts is an *oral text* and constitutes the integrity of the analysand's evidence in the clinical hour.'[13]

The narrative presentation is not the only ingredient in the clinical situation to be structured in this way. If we recall the analogy of the orchestral score, representing the multiple forms of communication that coexist during a session, it will be clear that we operate simultaneously within many different forms of sequential logic. Sequences of, for example, tones of voice, body expression, moods and emotions, will evolve throughout the session and will also be indicators of unconscious meaning. Bollas writes:

> Because of the nature of the dream-work – condensation, displacement, substitution, composites, and so forth – any unconscious idea

is going to travel through many different forms. It may be packed inside an image containing other ideas, displaced as an affect onto another 'innocent' thought, substituted by a stand-in, compromised by melding with another single object. To follow any logical chain means travelling along tracks that move through many different *forms* of representation. So, as an unconscious idea follows its sequential path, it moves in and out of various modes of articulation in order to complete itself.[14]

In *The Infinite Question* he explores a further issue. He describes how he had noticed increasingly in the course of his clinical work that patients will initiate the session with a question. This might be explicit or implicit, conscious or unconscious. Once the initial question has been posed, the patient's subsequent associations, though they may appear unrelated, often unconsciously provide an answer which, in turn, heralds a chain of further questions. Questioning can be anxious and obsessional or liberating and transformative; answers can be predictable and foreclosing or unexpected and generative. Any understanding is based on an implicit question, and this has a profound implication: that free association is a form of unconscious thinking.

Just as sound waves have different wavelengths, producing different pitches, the thematic threads of an analysis appear with varying periodicities. If the patient poses a complex question, some strands of meaning may wait until future sessions to become elaborated. Each person has her own psychic pace and thoughts will return to consciousness after the necessary unconscious work has been achieved. The same questions may recur many times during an analysis and they will spring different answers as time goes on. The mental jigsaw pieces may be around for a long time before the moment comes when they are organised into a picture that brings creative insight.

In music, too, we find that patterns of question and answer are everywhere, from the relationship between the smallest phrase fragments to the architectural structuring of whole movements or even complete works. (For an experience of a most profound emotional 'answer', think of the psychic impact of the final chorus of Bach's St Matthew Passion.) These variations of scale correspond to the varying periodicities of questions and answers as they appear in analytic material, from the interrelationship of adjacent verbal phrases to the meta-structure of an analysis as it evolves over several years.

Just as there would theoretically be no end point in the interpretation of a dream, the sequence of question and answer is also a potentially infinite process. Bollas writes: 'such questioning seems to be the drive behind the process of thought itself – as if, from the infantile moment until the time we die, we are in a state of endless questioning about our lives.'[15]

In Chapter 11 of *The Infinite Question*, Bollas illustrates this fundamental impulse by showing how two seminal dramas, *Oedipus Rex* and *Hamlet*, are driven throughout by question after question. He maintains that these great plays epitomise the way in which our mind works. Sophocles and Shakespeare are both asking, essentially: what do I know that has not yet been thought? Bollas writes: 'the force of questioning resides in the pressure brought to bear on the mind to think unthought knowledge.'[16]

It seems, therefore, that the logic of question and answer (related to the epistemophilic drive) is an intrinsic form, a template in the human psyche that is of itself formative and creative, preceding, and irrespective of, any specific conceptual referrant. Bollas suggests that it originates in infancy, as the baby starts to become aware of the gulf between the maternal mind and his own. A sense of bewilderment at things that we cannot consciously encompass stays with us, epitomised by the intriguing and puzzling experience of the dream. He maintains that as we grow towards old age we become less invested in finding solutions, and more intrigued by the realisation that the questioning process can never be made redundant by answers.

So far we have considered some of the many forms of communication present in free associative material. Although immensely valuable for the unconscious contents this reveals, Bollas also sees the *process* of free association as therapeutic in itself, as mentally formative for both patient and analyst. It develops unconscious capabilities, and this, for him, constitutes the most profound and central aim of psychoanalytic treatment.

But can this technique be expected to work in all circumstances? Can a patient who is severely disturbed really free associate?

Bollas does indeed maintain that Freud's method can, and should, form the basis of psychoanalytic work with all types of pathology. Just as the 'normal' neurotic patient will find his conscious theories about himself loosened by his associative discoveries, the simple process of speaking in detail about everyday life can provide a counterpoint to the pathological mechanisms that are keeping the severely ill patient imprisoned. Bollas writes: 'The therapeutic genius of this method is that it quite naturally breaks down the paralysing authority of any symptom or pathological structure.'[17]

Let us start with borderline pathology. The borderline person's internal experience is generally founded on the pursuit of turbulent difference with her objects. The invitation to recount the events of her ordinary life can enrage her, because such issues feel like an irrelevant diversion. She prefers to reiterate her theory about how badly the world treats her, and to present generalisations that serve to corroborate her core grievance. However, if the analyst quietly persists in encouraging her to speak specifically and in detail about her life, the patient will start, in spite of herself, to be in touch with islands of ordinary creativity in the ego, and this will gradually facilitate the formation of new, less contaminated internal objects – in other words, the beginnings of psychic genera. As she is encouraged to listen to her own associations, she will start to relinquish her exclusive addiction to a toxic internal world and become more able to inhabit her environment. Gradually she acquires a place to stand in order to begin the work of analytic exploration.

Bollas suggests that the schizophrenic patient experiences the repeated disappearance of his being. This is a life lived within a fragmented form of dream logic that can seem to others to be meaningless. In fact the patient is speaking directly from the unconscious, but he is unable to reflect on what he says, and so may have no access to understanding the sense of his words.

In this situation Bollas maintains that it is vital to listen particularly closely to what the schizophrenic patient is actually saying. By interrupting the flow of psychotic speech to comment in detail on what the patient has just said, the analyst shows him that his ideas are in fact of intense interest, and moreover, that they can be thought about. By helping the patient to listen to himself in this way, the non-psychotic parts of the mind become capable of secondary process thinking that is recognised by both participants, and in this way he gradually starts to decode some of the meaning that is encrypted within his apparent madness.

In the case of manic depressive illness, Bollas regards it as a priority to help the patient reconnect with the specific life events that precipitated breakdown and to reintroduce him to the ordinary logic of his history, his relationships and responsibilities. Rather like the borderline, the manic person will resist this, dismissing it as mundane and irrelevant. However, insisting on detail helps to slow the manic episode down, rooting the patient back into his everyday world. This facilitates the return of the split-off depressive aspects of the personality and thus reduces the intensity of the mania.

In the depressive phase of the illness, the patient experiences a deadening loss of agency, and there will be a profound reluctance to rouse himself to describe the details of ordinary life. However, if the analyst gently insists on the examination of lived experience, this reinstates links with the external world and reduces the depressive focus on withdrawal and self-punishment.

In all these situations, the analyst is demonstrating absorbed and differentiated listening, proving that he is immersed in aspects of the patient's life that the patient himself is discounting. The analyst-as-listener gradually becomes internalised, and the unconscious meanings inherent in the patient's words grow into a shared vocabulary of knowledge and understanding. By persisting in encouraging free association, the analyst helps the patient to see what is ordinary in apparently extraordinary states of mind, and this helps to break the stranglehold of psychotic thinking.

As we associate to dreams, memories and current life events, we arrive at present insights but we also sow the seeds of future explorations. Once again it is a matter of form versus content: however significant the individual moments of realisation, these will always be secondary to the invaluable process of continually re-forming and expanding our understanding, liberating us from the mental foreclosure of certainty.

This approach enables the patient to expand her relationship with the network of associated ideas in her mind, only occasionally narrowing the focus when there is something specific – it might be a symptom, an element of character pathology or a transference enactment – that is ready to be understood. If she can explore her associations without being restricted by premature meanings, this allows her to develop an awareness of, and a curiosity about, the complexity of her internal world. This way of working reflects Bollas's core trust, not only in the wisdom of the patient's unconscious, but in the value of the analyst's capacity to respond unconsciously.

The patient who is immersed in the analytic process often looks forward to his sessions with a mixture of anxiety, curiosity and anticipation, and the expansive experience of discovering new connections with the unconscious can feel deeply creative. Bollas describes an intrinsic *pleasure* in the freedom to articulate the internal world, something that is well known to psychoanalysts and analysands but rarely discussed. The fact that the creative elaboration of idiom feels pleasurable in itself challenges the Kleinian notion that creativity evolves in order to make unconscious reparation for damage. In Bollas's terms, creativity does not presuppose guilt; what it presupposes is the quest for transformation of the self. In 'Creativity and psychoanalysis' (MT), he writes:

> Entering analysis a person will never be the same again. He will have found a new object for self transformation and there is nothing like it, just as there is nothing like painting, nothing like poetry and nothing like music.[18]

Notes

1 Bollas, C. 'The goals of psychoanalysis?', MT pp.68–9.
2 Freud, S. (1923) 'Two encyclopaedia articles', *The Complete Psychological Works of Sigmund Freud, ed. Strachey, J. (London: Hogarth) XVIII.*
3 Bollas, C. 'Introduction', MT p.2.
4 Bollas, C. 'Free association', EOW pp.8–9 (original italics).
5 Bollas, C. 'Introduction', MT p.1.
6 Bollas, C. 'Free association', EOW pp.37–8.
7 Bollas, C. 'Dissemination', CU p.53.
8 Bollas, C. *The Infinite Question*, p.135.
9 Molino, A. (ed.) (1997) *Freely Associated: Encounters in Psychoanalysis.* London: Free Association Books, pp.22–3.
10 Bollas, C. 'Dissemination', CU p.61.
11 Bollas, C. 'Normotic illness', SO pp.154–5.
12 Freud, S. (1933a) 'New introductory lectures on psycho-analysis', *SE XXII.*
13 Bollas, C. 'Articulations of the unconscious', FM p.57 (original italics).
14 Bollas, C. *The Infinite Question*, p.10 (original italics).
15 Ibid., p.22.
16 Ibid., p.144.
17 Bollas, C. 'Introduction', MT p.2.
18 Bollas, C. 'Creativity and psychoanalysis', MT p.176.

Chapter 10

The Freudian Pair

Key papers

'Off the wall' (FD)
'The psychoanalyst's use of free association' (BC)
'Communications of the unconscious' (CU)
'Transference interpretation as a resistance to free association' (FM)
'The necessary destructions of psychoanalysis' (MT)

Key concepts: *the dialectics of difference; simple and complex self states*

The topic of the analytic relationship is addressed from many angles throughout Bollas's writings. This chapter will consider some of the implications of his theoretical ideas for the unique partnership that he terms *The Freudian Pair* – the relationship created when the free associating patient meets the evenly hovering attention of the analyst. Bollas describes this as 'the revolutionary discovery of a new object relation'.[1]

All the aspects of his metapsychological model come together in the consulting room: the receptive unconscious and psychic genera, the elaboration of idiom via the selection and use of objects, the infinite complexity of the unconscious, the presentation and representation of self, and the unique potential of free association. The analytic relationship also incorporates the various dualities that underpin his thinking: maternal and paternal, subjective and objective, dissemination and focus, form and content.

Bollas makes it clear to the new patient that psychoanalysis will be a joint effort:

> I think it is an important part of the therapeutic alliance for the analyst to point out to the analysand how he or she is creating the analysis. However important the analyst's role, it is ultimately dependent

on what the patient creates. Most analysands are oblivious to their own creativity. By reflecting upon their many lines of thought we indicate to the analysand how rich a source of thinking he or she really is.[2]

In Chapter 6 we discussed Bollas's concept of *interformality*. A subtle, unconscious restructuring of both selves takes place in any encounter between two people, and the collaborative relationship of the Freudian Pair is no exception. Although the analytic session is based on the free associations of the patient, the process operates *between* analyst and patient. As well as being absorbed in the patient's narratives, dreams, history and conflicts, the analyst is also involved in a more subtle kind of intimacy: the direct effect of the patient's presentation of self. Bollas writes:

> there is another type of knowing, the work of 'in-formation', as one person's particular character affects the other as an idiom of presentation. So there is the knowledge of content and I can describe what my patient said when he told me about his dream. I cannot, however, describe the idiom or style of presentation. You would have to have been there to have experienced it yourself. For this knowledge is mostly unthinkable and unrepresentable.[3]

The themes that are addressed consciously will be driven by innumerable threads of psychic interest, and understanding will be the result of a parallel, mutually responsive internal discourse within the two participants. The patient will sense this unconscious intersubjectivity through the details of the analyst's response, which will depend on an intuitive sense of what to say, how to phrase things and when to remain silent.

According to the forming aesthetic of his own personality and his growing perception of the patient's idiom, the analyst develops a genre specific to each individual. He learns how to speak in a way that is usable by that particular patient's receptive intelligence. Bollas points out that, especially when dealing with someone who has been severely developmentally deprived, it is often not the analysis of mental contents that is most crucial, but the *experience* of ideas and feelings being transformed into words – idiom being given form.

There is an educative dimension to his approach. At times it is helpful for the patient if she can develop a sense of the way the analyst's mind is at work on the psychoanalytic task. If he indicates the thought processes that have led him to an interpretation, this illustrates something about the free, creative use of the mind. It also demonstrates the limits of the analyst's understanding, counteracting illusions of omniscience.

Bollas emphasises the dangers inherent in the analyst assuming the role of *telling* the patient the unconscious meaning of her communications, and he advocates counteracting this by, at times, openly representing the function of not knowing. This works against the authoritarian situation that, consciously or unconsciously, is almost bound to be an assumption in the patient's expectations. The patient both fears and desires an omniscient analyst, but in the end this is constricting, and far less valuable than the experience of being educated by her own mind.

Some unconscious lines of thought lead to areas of repression – hidden sexual and aggressive ideas that are censored by the ego – and it is an inherently humiliating experience to become aware of one's habitual defences and everyday self-deceptions. However, Bollas suggests that it will be less difficult for the patient to accept these aspects of herself if she perceives them not as information presented by a powerful parental other, but as originating from her own unconscious communications.

In fact, basing the analysis on free association in itself subverts the idea that understanding originates in the mind of the analyst. Bollas writes: 'Freudian reflection is deeply respectful of the specific contents of the patient's mind, their own unique logic of thought, and their precise words.'[4]

Where necessary, he will acknowledge the very real possibility that what he has said may be mistaken. If the analyst is open with the patient when he realises that he has made a mistake, this creates a new space, allowing the potential for unthought knowledge to arrive. It also reduces the patient's anxiety about saying something that is not quite right. This analytic approach helps to reduce authoritarianism, but it also models the analyst's relationship to his own subjectivity. He is demonstrating that, in the same way as the patient's associations are considered, his own ideas can also be thought about.

Another related aspect of technique that encourages a free, fluid atmosphere is what Bollas terms *the dialectics of difference*. In 'Off the wall' (FD), he describes how he will explicitly give the patient the right, and the opportunity, to differ with him; to disagree with, or modify, what is being suggested without this automatically being treated as evidence of resistance. In a relaxed and undramatic way, this establishes ordinary difference as a non-traumatic and essential factor in the analysis and, by extension, in mental life in general.

Bollas maintains that this democratic stance does not interfere with the patient's projective or transferential uses of the analyst – these are

powerful unconscious mechanisms that will not be prevented from operating. However, it can be useful in helping to manage situations that
might otherwise become stuck, such as a potentially malignant regression or an intense transference neurosis that is restricting rather than fur-
thering analytic process.

Establishing the category of difference also models the developmental stage of *perceptive identification* (discussed in Chapter 7), in which
the capacity to perceive the object as separate deepens and enriches the
potential of the relationship. This function can be impeded by a highly
interpretive technique, and it is one of the ways in which such an approach
can be infantalising. Bollas writes:

> there can be no perceptive identification if the analyst or therapist
> intervenes before the analysand is able to establish his narrative,
> affective, and character identity in the session. Such early interven-
> tions are the stuff of projective identification when the analyst feels
> he knows what is going on right away.[5]

The principal task of the Freudian Pair is to facilitate the expression of
unconscious thinking. There will be times when important work is going
on internally without either person understanding consciously what it is,
especially if the patient is immersed in a process of unconscious elaboration. The functions performed by the free associating patient and the
free listening analyst become structuralised over time, so consciousness
becomes the 'other' for the unconscious, and vice versa.

Bollas points out that every patient is, as Freud himself was at the
start of his explorations, both the object of the investigation and the
subject undertaking the enquiry. However, as he listens to the patient
the analyst, too, finds himself returned to the Freudian position of self-
analysis. Freud proposed a technique that sponsors unconscious creativity in both participants, and this requires a fluidity in the analyst's
mind. Rather than confining himself to his conceptual understandings,
which can never be more than the tip of the iceberg, he allows himself
to expand into the condensed, symbolic and overdetermined world of
unconscious thinking. Bollas writes: 'the act of psychoanalysis and the
analytic relationship will always be derivatives of the unthought known
resident in each.'[6]

As unconscious communication enables the analyst to tune in to the
patient's idiom, receiving her latent trains of thought, the two participants develop a joint capacity for unconscious thinking. Bollas maintains that in order to function in this way, analysts need to increase their

unconscious capabilities and to be content to postpone conscious understanding. Just as the patient is asked not to prearrange an agenda, the
analyst must avoid selective listening so as to be open to unconscious
communication. If he is waiting to pounce on the occasional slip of the
tongue or is automatically on the lookout for transference manifestations,
he will not be free to receive the patient's flow of ideas, with their multiple lines of psychic interest. Bollas writes:

> Freud's innovative method of listening honours this complexity and
> encourages the analyst to meet the analysand in an intermediate area
> in which they share something of the same frame of mind.
>   The issues of practice arising from this technique are demand-
> ing. In the first place, both participants have to give up the under-
> standable wish to 'make sense' of what is being said as the session
> proceeds.[7]

But how do we know that the analyst is truly in a state of attuned reverie
and not just hazily out of touch?

In 'Off the wall' (FD), Bollas discusses the difference between a state
of mental vagueness that represents a lack of expertise, and the more
demanding, not-knowing frame of mind that is 'a necessary condition for
the creation of a potential space, an analytic screen that we sustain and
which registers the patient's idiom'.[8] He suggests that the best indicator
of analytic attunement is the patient's reaction. If she responds to the analyst's comments, not merely with a foreclosing response of agreement or
dismissal but with a flowering of new associative material, this indicates
the presence of unconscious communication.

The Freudian Pair operate in both the maternal and paternal orders, and
this duality is symbolised in the time frame of the session. Bollas writes:

> Psychoanalysis operates from and between the maternal and paternal
> orders, which are present simultaneously in the bound and unbound
> temporality of the analytic hour. The session is time-limited, thus
> according with the laws of the paternal: father time. But within this
> bound temporality that are portals through which the self is trans-
> ported to the infinite temporality of the maternal.[9]

For the most part, the analyst's mode of listening is receptive rather
than explanatory. As reasoned thought dissolves into associative thinking, the Freudian Pair are returned to something close to the atmosphere

of the maternal dyad. This is implied by Freud's famous instructions to the analyst:

> Experience soon showed that the attitude which the analytic physician could most advantageously adopt was to surrender himself to his own unconscious mental activity, in a state of *evenly suspended attention*, to avoid as far as possible reflection and the construction of conscious expectations, not to try to fix anything he heard particularly in his memory, and by these means to catch the drift of the patient's unconscious with his own unconscious.[10]

At some point, patient and analyst will emerge into the paternal order to engage in articulating and exploring the unconscious experience they have shared. They will then make use of separation, differentiation and structure to gain conscious understanding. The carefully considered interpretation, arrived at after much gathering together of unconscious threads, will be overdetermined – the result of a process of condensation in the analyst's mind.

In this way, maternal and paternal come together to produce integrated growth. Bollas suggests that, just as in the early stages of life, the maternal must precede the paternal:

> What is needed is an initial experience of successive ego transformations that are identified with the analyst and the analytic process. In such moments, the patient experiences interpretations primarily for their capacity to match his internal mood, feeling or thought, and such moments of rapport lead the patient to 're-experience' the transformational object relation.[11]

I have found that one of the most frequent misconceptions about Bollas's work is the idea that he does not use the transference. In view of his extensive focus on free association this is perhaps not surprising, but it is far from the truth.

His approach to transference is in fact highly nuanced and subtle. He points out that in looking at a piece of clinical material we may immediately notice evidence of the patient's predominant transference to the analyst, but at the same time her associations will often reveal other, more subtle transference patterns that are more deeply unconscious. He suggests that if the analyst is open to these it reduces the temptation to dwell repetitively on a single transferential theme.

He regards transference not as axiomatically pre-eminent in importance, but as integrated within the complexity of the unconscious:

> While transference is an order that takes place *all* the time, the fact that *it is there* does not mean that it subsumes into itself all the other orders and their categories of unconscious thinking. As discussed, Freud never envisioned the transference in this way. The transference could be 'unobjectionable', which means that nothing of unconscious significance was operating there. The patient might be using the analyst's mind to assist his own unconscious process of thought. This is use of the object. Transference is a *form* of thinking.[12]

For Bollas, one of the primary tasks of psychoanalysis is to enable an expansion in the patient's curiosity about, and enjoyment of, her own unconscious complexity. This involves the ability to make flexible, varied use of the analyst. The freedom to be complex will depend to a significant extent on the individual's experience of the primary relationship, and this will be brought into the analytic situation via the transference. If the mother has not provided the infant with sufficient transformational experiences, the patient may be limited in her capacity to use the analyst in creative and differentiated ways.

Freud describes the psychoanalytic relationship as consisting of a free associating patient and an evenly suspended analyst. Just as importantly, however, the activity of the Freudian Pair will involve the *analyst's* free associations and the *patient's* freedom to be in a state of reverie.

In considering this unique relationship, Bollas returns to another duality related to the maternal and paternal orders: the oscillation between simple and complex self states. In 'The psychoanalyst's use of free association' (BC), he explores a balance that is needed in the analyst between a position of subjectivity, a mode of self experiencing in which his unconscious is allowed to engage with the material in an unmediated way, and an objective mode that involves a complex, reflecting self.

In the category of subjectivity he includes the analyst's spontaneous responses – his associations, conjectures, fleeting ideas, feelings and hunches. As well as governing the formulation of interpretations, the objective mode includes all the structuring elements in the clinical situation, such as moral neutrality, consistency, sensitivity to the patient's response to interpretations, awareness of her understanding of her personal history (inevitably a mixture of myth and reconstruction), and the monitoring of the transference and the quality of wider object relations conveyed by aspects of the dialogue. Importantly, Bollas also includes the privileging of the patient's right to free association.

Here he describes the oscillation between different self states in, and between, patient and analyst:

> It is a dialectic operating between two different mental dispositions, as the participants exchange the positions of simple and complex self. One moment the analysand lost in narrative thought is accompanied by his analyst, who is also immersed in the experience of listening. Another moment the analyst moves to a reflective, complex-self position before reassuming the experiencing state. On occasion the analyst is in a simple-self state, following trains of inner associative logic, while the patient is objectifying himself, perhaps telling the analyst what he thinks his prior associations mean.[13]

He points out that, in certain respects, the analyst's associations can be freer than those of the patient. Absorbed in shifting self states, fragments of daydream and fluctuating feelings, he will sometimes find himself dwelling on a detail of the narrative when the story has moved on. Whereas the patient has the task of organising her thoughts and feelings into words, the analyst is permitted, rather paradoxically, to be less coherent. For much of the time he can remain quietly within his own receptive, imaginative internal world.

As we explored in Chapter 8, Bollas shows how our minds move continually between a concentrated state of psychic focus, and a disseminated mode in which there is a diffuse expansion of the self. Each state depends for its potential on the other, and psychic health requires the capacity to alternate freely between the two. This oscillation is present, moment to moment, in our ordinary subjectivity; it manifests in the subjective experience of both participants in the Freudian Pair; and it is a necessary element in the analyst's technique. He requires the ability to utilise both an expansive, free associative state and an objective, synthesising position in which he can gather his understandings into an interpretation.

In 'The necessary destructions of psychoanalysis' (MT), Bollas relates this duality to another, familiar psychoanalytic pairing: 'This destruction is the joint work of the death instinct, breaking up links in order to reduce excitation, and the life instinct, creating new combinations of thought.'[14] And, in the following passage he brings in the theory of psychic genera:

> The work of an analysis operates between this binary opposition. Faced with vast areas of material, a part of the analyst is comparatively free

of mind to respond, yet another part of him searches for the organising nuclei of psychic truths. A single word, a phrase, an image, or the memory of a previous session will feel weighty with meaning. As time passes a small psychic chamber fills up with these denser objects and suddenly in a moment's illumination the analyst sees why they join; out of this genera an interpretation arises.[15]

Simple and complex intrapsychic modes represent different forms of desire. One is the wish to inhabit the idiom of the self; the other is the drive to satisfy the epistemophilic instinct – the urge to know.

There can be a natural ambivalence in the analyst about revealing to colleagues the unique, intimate relationship of the Freudian Pair. We have already noted that in any clinical account much more will be left out than can be reported, and the simple-self state of direct, unmediated experience is especially hard to convey. Although in a clinical discussion the elucidation of meaning and the quest for precise understanding may be laudable endeavours, it is closer to the reality of the situation to accept that, for much of the time, analyst and patient are immersed in a web of shifting meanings. The analyst who can allow himself to be lost in the process may not win prizes for conceptual clarity, but he will be of profound value to the patient.

Notes

1   Bollas, C. 'Psychic transformations', FM p.13.
2   Bollas, C. 'Articulations of the unconscious', FM p.56.
3   Bollas, C. 'The place of the psychoanalyst', MT p.26.
4   Bollas, C. 'The mystery of things', MT p.186.
5   Bollas, C. 'Perceptive identification', FM p.67.
6   Bollas, C. *China on the Mind*, p.64.
7   Bollas, C. *The Infinite Question*, p.20.
8   Bollas, C. 'Off the wall', FD p.62.
9   Bollas, C. *China on the Mind*, p.61.
10 Freud, S. (1923) 'Two encyclopaedia articles', *The Complete Psychological works of Sigmund Freud, ed. Strachey, J. (London: Hogarth) XIX* p.239 (original italics).
11 Bollas, C. 'The transformational object', SO p.23.
12 Bollas, C. 'Articulations of the unconscious', FM p.52 (original italics).
13 Bollas, C. 'The psychoanalyst's use of free association', BC p.106.
14 Bollas, C. 'The necessary destructions of psychoanalysis', MT p.27.
15 Ibid., p.34.

Chapter 11

Worlds apart

Key papers

'Ordinary regression to dependence' (SO)
'On transference interpretation as a resistance to free association' (FM)
'Psychic transformations' (FM)
'What is theory?' (FM)
'Perceptive identification' (FM)
'Historical sets and the conservative process' (FD)
'The mystery of things' (MT)
China on the Mind

Key concepts: *theoretical pluralism; theories as forms of perception; historical sets*

Bollas's metapsychology offers a distinctive model of the structure and functioning of the mind. Alongside this, however, he makes a powerful argument for theoretical pluralism.

All our various psychoanalytic theories enable us to conceptualise particular aspects of the mind that might otherwise remain unconscious and unthought, and each offers concepts that are relevant for understanding particular elements of our experience. Thus, as we saw in Chapter 2, repression is best conceptualised using the spatial metaphor of Freud's topographical model, whereas psychic development and the conflictual dynamics within the mind are most usefully approached with the more anthropomorphic structural model. Without the full range of psychoanalytic theories we would be unable to think about certain sorts of phenomena.

However, in 'What is theory?' (FM), where he explores the status and the limitations of psychoanalytic ideas, Bollas suggests that a theory provides something even more fundamental than a way of thinking. He writes that theories are '*forms of perception*'.[1] Just as we use our various physical senses to register different aspects of external reality, psychoanalysts need all their theoretical concepts because each allows them to perceive phenomena in a way that the others do not. If their conceptual repertoire lacks theories such as, for example, Freud's Oedipus complex, Klein's paranoid-schizoid and depressive positions, or Winnicott's transitional phenomena, there will be things happening in the consulting room that they simply will not see.

Just as the clinician's theories affect how he perceives and conceptualises his patients, they also shape the way he works with them, and Bollas warns against an over-preoccupation with any theoretical viewpoint. Seeing the patient through a single lens will obscure the complexity of the mind and its communications, and the analyst who is too wedded to a particular psychoanalytic orientation will be listening out for certain things in the material and will not be free to be absorbed in unconscious experience.

Bollas therefore advocates that the analyst immerse himself in as many different ways of thinking as possible, but he suggests that once he has familiarised himself thoroughly with a particular theory it should then be allowed to recede into the background of his mind, so that he is not governed by preconceptions connected with any particular model. The patient will unconsciously sense the range of awareness in the analyst. The broader this is, the more the therapeutic work has the potential to go beyond the analysis of pathology or character and to enable the patient to engage in free exploration of her unconscious mind.

In 'What is theory?', and more extensively in *China on the Mind*, Bollas contrasts the highly divergent approaches of the schools of thought that are predominant in modern British psychoanalysis. In what follows I shall bring together the main strands of his discussion and explore the place in this divided tradition of Bollas's own metapsychological model.

It is important to emphasise that in doing this I shall be addressing broad principles. It goes without saying that any individual psychoanalyst's work will be informed from many sources. He will have experienced a unique combination of influences, and he will have his preferred theories which he will approach in his own idiomatic way. However, if there appears to be a certain degree of caricature in what follows, I believe there is a value in generalising, in order to understand essential features of these orientations. They differ fundamentally – in their assumptions about the structure and functioning of the mind, in their approach to clinical technique and its rationale, and in their view of the therapeutic task.

From a metapsychological point of view, the Kleinian tradition is based upon a completely different view of mental life from the one proposed by Freud's dream theory and developed by Bollas. Instead of infinitely ramifying networks of associated ideas, constantly developing throughout life, Klein's model of the unconscious is that of a container populated with internal objects. It is an arena for the playing out of the drama of unconscious phantasies, and it is characterised by primitive drives and anxieties, the mechanisms of splitting and projection, and in particular by the struggle against the power of the death instinct. This produces a clinical emphasis on the nature of our internal objects, on our unconscious phantasies about what we do to them and what they might do to us, and on how these primitive object relationships are reflected and recreated in the here-and-now experience with the analyst.

Although the insights gained by these explorations are indisputable – and Bollas undoubtedly values many of the theoretical ideas that have come from the Kleinian tradition – it is no secret that he takes issue with a technique based on frequent interpretation of the transference. He alludes to this throughout his writings, but his most fundamental objections are presented, in no uncertain terms, in 'On transference interpretation as a resistance to free association' (FM). This paper can come as a shock – its no-holds-barred flavour is clear from its title – but if Bollas occasionally exaggerates to make his points, they are points that confront us with very real differences.

Compared with the basically receptive Freudian stance, Kleinian technique is more actively interpretive, and Bollas discusses various senses in which this can be antithetical to free association.

The analytic patient is asked to resist the temptation to arrive at her session with a conscious agenda, but he points out that the analyst whose mind has been trained to focus on the transference will have an agenda of his own: a preconception of what he expects to hear. He will therefore be liable to interrupt the unfolding of the patient's narrative sooner rather than later, steering her attention towards what is of most interest to him. If she is not given space the patient will be unable to talk freely, and if her unconscious is not permitted to choose the trajectory of the material, neither participant can know how it might have developed over the course of the session.

In this situation, the Freudian attitude of evenly hovering attention becomes superseded by the task of translating meaning, understanding becomes reductive rather than expansive, and the patient loses the crucial freedom to follow an exploratory sequence of unconscious logic. Bollas insists that elucidating the transference does not equate with understanding mental complexity: 'the deep work of the unconscious is ended with the brisk work of interpreted relatedness.'[2]

Whereas the Freudian approach encourages the disseminated branching out of unconscious psychic interests, Klein's technique focuses on primitive relational dynamics and a concretisation of abstract ideas. Indeed, the more receptive, less interpretive Freudian form of listening is liable to be regarded by some as an avoidance of the immediacy of the patient's pathology.

If the material is continually related to the transference, the patient will infer that this issue has priority in the hierarchy of meaning. This technique can lead to a stuck situation in which a predominant transference pattern is repeatedly interpreted while other aspects of the patient's life and mind remain excluded. The translation of the narrative into a metaphor for the analytic relationship can seem to offer a tempting resolution to confusion and ambiguity. It promotes cure by means of a quasi-parental relationship and a narrative restructuring in which the complexity of the self is boiled down to core object relational principles. Bollas writes: 'the Transference becomes *the solution* to the question of the analysand's unconscious.'[3]

As well as interfering with the patient's capacity for free association, he maintains that this way of working fundamentally contradicts the essential primacy of *unconscious* processes. Although Kleinian analysts certainly use the concept of unconscious communication, their view of this is governed predominately by the mechanism of projective identification, understood in terms of a defensive acting upon objects.

As we have seen, Bollas regards the issue of unconscious expression much more broadly. In the following passage, which refers to many of the elements discussed in Chapters 8 and 9, he outlines the scope of the subtle, many-faceted communications offered by the patient's narrative:

> The crucial early words of a session, the unconscious selection of topics, the patterns of ideas that reveal themselves (eventually) through the movement from one topic to another, the ring of certain phrases, the evocative and ramifying effect of a single word, the far-reaching suggestion of a metaphor.[4]

A technique based on tracking closely what the patient is saying and making frequent interpretations relies on the assumption that the *conscious* mind of the analyst is capable of following the latent significance of the patient's narrative. This limits the potential of the analyst's use of his own unconscious, privileging mechanisms of projection and introjection at the expense of receptive and evocative functions. The concept of the Freudian Pair in a state of mutual reverie is lost, and Bollas goes as far as to say that this active approach can actually *prevent* unconscious communication from taking place.

The patient who repeatedly hears her analyst translating the meaning of her words will come to expect explanations and to regard them as being the point of the analysis. She will also start to assume that the 'answers' lie in the mind of the analyst. This will intensify the transferential relationship, and the patient may become so preoccupied with this dynamic that she opts out of the basic task of speaking about her life. Transference interpretations can become a powerfully containing story. For some people this is gratifying; for others it will be constricting and mentally claustrophobic. If this intense pseudo-intimacy with the analyst comes at the expense of free talking, the patient will be denied the opportunity to experience the expansive potential inherent in her own unconscious.

Far from being a democratic joint effort, when this situation goes wrong it can result in a traumatic imbalance of power. If the analyst becomes a harsh superego figure in the patient's mind, she will easily feel judged and reproached, and may well be too anxious to be able to free associate. Here, Bollas describes a worst case scenario:

> I have no doubt that such a listening perspective collapses the analysand's wish to be unconsciously communicative. This may lead the analysand to retreat into an enclave in order to ward off the intense intrusiveness of the analyst. Such a retreat is seen by the analyst as evidence of the invidiously destructive ambition of the analysand's negative transference, and is a profound tragedy in my view: for the analysand, but also for psychoanalysis.[5]

The implications of these issues are profound. Comparing the Freudian and Kleinian approaches, Bollas writes:

> They differ in the type of mentality that invites the patient's unconscious participation. They differ in the fate of the patient's unconscious participation in the session. They differ in their orientations to the visual and the verbal orders, or the imaginary and the symbolic. They differ in their conceptions of analytical time and space. They differ in the after-effects of an analysis.[6]

As we have discussed, Bollas certainly regards the transference as a highly significant element in the therapeutic situation. However, he supports the distinction between interpreting the transference and working *within* it. A particular manifestation of the transference relationship may be obvious, but he may choose not to interpret it explicitly in terms of what the patient is doing at that moment, as this can provoke excitement and an intensification of feeling that can disrupt the natural flow of associations. He believes that working within the transference avoids the trap of repeatedly confronting the patient with one particular aspect of her internal world. This reduces the danger of authoritarianism and it demonstrates an inherent respect for the patient, allowing her the freedom to use the transferential aspects of the analytic relationship fluidly and creatively, without feeling confronted, accused or trapped.

Within British psychoanalytic training the emphasis on the transference has become an unquestioned assumption. (I cannot have been the only anxious trainee to have had the guilty thought: 'I've got a clinical seminar tomorrow – I'd better make a transference interpretation.') This has led to a situation in which the principal therapeutic aim has shifted, from the use of free association to explore the complexity of the unconscious mind to the reworking of the dynamics of the patient's primary relationships. Rather than being regarded as one important element in a wider picture, the transference has become the new defining feature of psychoanalysis.

Bollas's critique of Kleinian technique is powerful, and it will be clear by now that his own approach has both a different rationale and very different therapeutic priorities. On the other hand, in certain respects the flavour of his clinical writing has much in common with Winnicott's, and it often attracts readers for similar reasons.

Winnicott advocated a dreamy, unintegrated state of reverie that reflected the merged, holding nature of the primitive maternal dyad. For him, the predominant aim was to enable the emergence of the true self. In order to facilitate this he would create a benign, nurturing relationship that fostered regression as a central therapeutic tool.

Just as he acknowledges the importance of appropriate work in the transference, Bollas recognises the therapeutic value, at times, of a state of benign regression. Indeed, he describes his training analysis with Masud Khan, which he valued greatly, as a predominantly regressive experience, and his early paper 'Ordinary regression to dependence' (SO) is a sensitive and imaginative contribution to this way of working.

However, in *China on the Mind* he makes a radical statement. He suggests that, although in many ways it inhabits the opposite end of the psychoanalytic spectrum from Kleinian technique, the Winnicottian approach, too, represents a significant departure from Freud's original vision.

Unlike Klein, Winnicott would wait in silence for long periods in order to encourage the dismantling of the patient's false self-defences and the emergence of the true self. Unlike Freud, he did not require the patient to put his internal world into words. He was not primarily concerned with the *meaning* of the latent contents; in fact he tended to regard wide-ranging verbal associations as a defence against the essential formlessness of human existence. Here, Bollas encapsulates this difference:

> In a Freudian analysis an image is a concentration of possible words. Speaking will unpack the image, as words express latent meanings with a chain of signifiers. In a Winnicottian analysis the image arrives out of nowhere, seemingly from outside the self. It is a moment in time. It carries weight, yet it is evanescent and without articulated significance. It is not to be spoken, as to do so would be to recognise its separateness from the self.[7]

Bollas claims that a treatment based on the recreation of early self states, although it may be profoundly moving and potentially therapeutic, cannot be essentially *analytic* because it fails to acquaint the patient with an understanding of the ingredients of her mind. By privileging the pre-verbal maternal order, the Winnicottian analyst therefore deprives the patient of the unique potential of free association as a means of exploring the unconscious. In addition, this approach is liable to result in profound dependence on the analyst – not because the patient is in thrall to an omniscient parental figure who tells her what she means, but because she is merged into a primitive quasi-maternal dyad.

Bollas suggests that, if taken to extremes, neither the Kleinian nor the Winnicottian approach will promote in the patient a mature, autonomous relationship with the unconscious and the capacity to live actively, creatively and independently in the external world. His reasoning implies that Winnicottian analysis can produce another worst-case scenario in which patients relinquish their sense of agency and remain permanently reliant on the analyst.

In his clinical work, Bollas undoubtedly makes selective use of both Kleinian and Winnicottian techniques. When a transference manifestation or enactment eclipses the work of free association and demands attention, he will interpret and analyse it as a significant communication from the patient's unconscious. He will also support the patient's right to regress temporarily into an unfocused state at moments when deep unconscious work is taking place. However, he aligns his own technique firmly with Freud's original project: to understand the unconscious mind by means of associative exploration that will reveal its complexity and its logical connections.

In order to facilitate this, he places great emphasis on the analyst's capacity to be quiet and receptive, not primarily to foster a primitive maternal environment, but to allow his own unconscious to be in-formed by the patient's idiom. In the following passage, he recognises the creative potential of a similar state in the patient:

> The receptive frame of mind is a conditional state; it depends on a relaxed, unvigilant attitude in the subject, and can be seen in analysands who are using silence to achieve an inner receptive orientation. From this position memories, daydreams, phantasies, and new internal objects are evoked. The analysand uses the analyst to hold the setting, to preserve the right of this frame of mind, and therefore is fundamentally unconcerned with the analyst as an object. Transference communicating is suspended. The ego is turned inward, to receive representations of internal psychic reality, and is not fundamentally engaged in projective-introjective dialectics with external objects and their internal representations.[8]

He frequently reminds us of Freud's emphasis on *unconscious* communication, and he makes it clear that this work cannot be rushed. In 'The mystery of things' (MT), he writes:

> This way of listening takes time, lots and lots of time. It takes time for the logic of sequence to be comprehended, it takes time for the evocative movement of the patient's discourse to affect the analyst's unconscious life. This aspect of an analysis leads to a greater appreciation of unconscious time and unconscious thought; indeed, it gives its participants a new appreciation of time itself.[9]

The analyst's state of evenly hovering attention requires him to relinquish the quest for immediate understanding. He must trust this and not be tempted to create premature meaning in an effort to provide the reassurance of certainty. For most of the time, the aim is to support the expansion of the patient's material rather than limiting or foreclosing it with explanation.

The analyst who is attuned to this level of communication might sometimes echo a particular word or image without knowing why, except that it resonates strikingly in his own mind. As the analysis develops, specific mental objects emerge as memorable; they coalesce into representations of unconscious lines of thought. These co-created analytic genera may acquire conscious meaning only very gradually, and sometimes they never become fully linked to consciousness. However, if the Freudian Pair is operating via the medium of free association, led by the patient, when the meaning of a chain of unconscious ideas does eventually emerge, the evidence will be clear to both participants: it will not be a conjectural meaning imposed from the outside.

As well as reinstating the centrality of free association, Bollas is also an advocate for the importance of the patient's relationship with her personal history. In their different ways, Klein and Winnicott both privilege early experience: Klein by focusing on early phantasied internal object relationships and Winnicott through the re-creation of the early maternal dyad. Both tend to ascribe less significance to the ongoing story of the patient's life. Indeed, the past tends to be relegated to 'reconstruction', a process regarded as secondary in therapeutic importance.

Bollas, on the other hand, gives explicit weight to the person's entire life experience. In 'Historical sets and the conservative process' (FD), he discusses the patient's changing relationship with her narrative about the past, giving importance both to recollection of actual experience and to elements of the story that are based on fantasy and the effects of *après-coup*.

His term *historical set* refers to a cluster of memories that relates to a particular epoch in the person's life, and is therefore anchored in a specific place and time. Some elements – the Oedipal set, the latency set, the adolescence set and so on – are developmental and universal. Others will relate to experiences unique to the individual. The creation of a historical set is not a simple act of reconstruction. It is psychically complex and overdetermined, the crystallisation of a significant existential moment that encapsulates a self state. Rather like the conservative mood, discussed in Chapter 4, the historical set is an act of preservation that includes retrospective reflection on the emotional reality of a particular era of life. It may not be a factually accurate memory, but it can be profoundly evocative and analytically informative.

For this dimension to be accessible to the analysis, the patient needs to *speak* about her past, freely and in great detail. This narrative will often change in the course of the analytic work as history is reworked and understood in many different ways. Bollas maintains that analysts who automatically treat recollection as a transference communication, and those who privilege the non-verbal state as the most profound form of communication, tend to neglect the psychic function of historical reflection. He maintains that the patient will sense the analyst's degree of interest in these aspects of her self experience, and may learn not to report them if she feels that their significance is negated. He writes:

> Historical thinking is a psychic accomplishment. It reflects an inner receptive area in the analyst that permits the analysand's development of a part of the psyche that stores self history. For me, it is important that the analyst possess a true historic consciousness, as this is a psychic function, not simply an intellectual stance. The function is an intelligent receptor of the patient's rememberings, which will be held by the analyst.[10]

Bollas's clinical thinking encompasses many of the theoretical discoveries of the Kleinian and Winnicottian traditions. However, his conception of the mind, in both its breadth and its detail, alters the emphasis of clinical psychoanalysis, always maintaining first and foremost a focus on the growth of unconscious capacities in the patient.

Notes

1   Bollas, C. 'What is theory?', FM p.77.
2   Bollas, C. 'The goals of psychoanalysis?', MT p.71.
3   Bollas, C. 'On transference interpretation as a resistance to free association', FM p.94 (original italics).
4   Bollas, C. 'Perceptive identification', FM pp.66–7.
5   Bollas, C. 'Psychic transformations', FM p.7.
6   Bollas, C. 'The mystery of things', MT p.189.
7   Bollas, C. *China on the Mind*, p.79.
8   Bollas, C. 'Historical sets and the conservative process', FD p.202.
9   Bollas, C. 'The mystery of things', MT pp.186–7.
10 Bollas, C. 'Historical sets and the conservative process', FD p.201.

Chapter 12

An integrated theory

The term *metapsychology* was coined by Freud in order to distinguish his creation, psychoanalysis, both from the classical psychologies of consciousness and from what he regarded as the delusional imaginings of metaphysics. It is an overarching term which brings together the fundamental concepts and principles that underpin his theoretical model of the mind.

Is it audacious to use this word to refer to Bollas's contribution?

I hope this book has shown that his many individual theoretical concepts do indeed add up to an integrated metapsychological model. Although its origins lie in aspects of Freud's revolutionary discoveries, it has its own emphases and it amounts to a unique theory of the mind.

Taking up his idea that theories are forms of perception, what does his model enable us to perceive? Do the concepts he offers provide us with new ways of thinking?

Bollas's espousal of theoretical plurality acknowledges the breadth of the human psyche. There are universal forces at work in all of us: instinctual development, the journey of infancy and the Oedipus complex, the adjustments to the demands of society in childhood and adolescence, and the various exigencies of the subsequent stages of adult life. These have been the focus for over a century of psychoanalytic exploration.

What Bollas contributes is a metapsychology that highlights the journey of the individual. He offers a theory that encompasses our motivation for curiosity about the world, and the unconscious mechanisms that govern the many-faceted interactions that take place, both within the self and in relation to external objects. In so doing, he enhances the psychoanalytical conception of what it is to be a human being.

His starting point is the highly sophisticated unconscious of Freud's dream theory, that selects elements of psychic significance from the experiences of the day, reshapes them by condensing, displacing and symbolising, and offers them to consciousness in a coded form, as the dream.

His most crucial addition to Freud's dreamwork model is the concept of idiom – the innate kernel of self. Although, as Freud shows, repression is undoubtedly a powerful ingredient, Bollas maintains that the character of our idiom is a more influential motivating force in the unconscious. It constitutes an underlying principle, a fundamental aesthetic that gives form to our individual experience, sponsoring the creative use of the environment and playing a crucial role in our relationships, both intrapsychic and external.

He offers ways of conceptualising aspects of the unconscious that were perceived by Freud but not extensively theorised by him, in particular the phenomena of unconscious perception, unconscious creativity and unconscious communication. The model of the receptive unconscious brings these elements into the foreground, providing a way of understanding their interrelationship and their centrality in the structure and functioning of the mind.

The work of psychic genera involves a continuous creative transformation of perceptions that are invited into the unconscious because they are of idiomatic interest. Genera operate not only within the individual mind; they can also be formed jointly between any two people who are in a close relationship. The unique intimacy of the psychoanalytic relationship – the Freudian Pair – leads to the creation of analytic genera which, over the course of an analysis, have their own creative trajectory, producing ramifying networks of associative complexity in the minds of both patient and analyst.

Bollas's view of our essential interrelationship with objects is another rich area of innovation. Aspects of external reality are selected and employed, both consciously and unconsciously, to elaborate our idiom, expanding and transforming self experience through moments of aesthetic intensity. This involves not only projective activity, but also the structuring effects on us of the intrinsic integrity of the object-in-itself.

Above all, Bollas insists on the primacy of unconscious processes. His theory that we are constantly in-formed by the idiom of the other offers a way of conceptualising the issue of unconscious communication. Alongside the conscious content of our lives – the many ways in which we think and talk about ourselves and our experiences – our essential form, and its manifestation through the unconscious effects of character, will always constitute the most profound kind of communication. However exhaustively we may be analysed, we never lose our psychic fingerprint and its unique effect upon the other.

The most fundamental relationship we have is the relationship between our conscious and unconscious selves. The various related dualities that permeate Bollas's thinking put us in touch with an underlying balance in human experience, one that applies equally to moment-to-moment subjective experience and to the overall structure of a personality. He continually reminds us that the most significant communications happen at the level of form rather than content.

What are the implications of Bollas's metapsychology for the tasks, and the goals, of psychoanalysis?

The various psychoanalytic traditions privilege different areas of theoretical thinking – instincts, object relations, true self spontaneity, empathy, transference – that produce a variety of therapeutic aims. For Bollas, each of these elements plays its part, but he regards psychoanalysis as having a wider and more inclusive aspiration: the exploration of the unconscious as a whole.

The intricacies of subjective and intersubjective experience present us with an infinitely complex vista, and he insists that our clinical technique should reflect, enable and honour this complexity. Psychoanalysis – analysis of the *mind* – should not be reduced to the analysis of symptoms, relationships or the experiences of early life. Important though these elements are, allowing any single aspect to dictate the scope of an analysis would be akin to examining one architectural feature of a house but never stepping back to appreciate the building as a whole.

His insistence that it is the unconscious of the patient and not the theories of the analyst that must steer the course of an analysis brings him back to Freud's initial discovery of the therapeutic use of free association, with its focus on the latent logic of the patient's narrative. From many points of view, Bollas shows how this approach enables the patient to inhabit a transformative space that liberates the intrinsic creativity of the unconscious.

His vision of the scope of psychoanalysis can be fully appreciated only if it is related to his metapsychology as a whole: the receptive unconscious with its structure of continuously developing psychic genera, the intricate interplay of idiom with evocative objects, the multiplicity of self states, the many categories of unconscious communication, and the pervasive presence of the unthought known.

Psychoanalysts have written rather little about what constitutes health. They take it as read, perhaps. For Bollas, however, the image of the healthy creative mind underpins his understanding of every aspect of clinical work, and he emphasises the importance of allowing the well-functioning parts of the patient into the consulting room. His therapeutic aim therefore transcends the absence of pathology. In regarding the elaboration of idiom as the driving force of the self, he is postulating an intrinsic purpose, a sense of future in the individual, and this, he maintains, should be recognised and supported by psychoanalysis.

Bollas's metapsychology offers a comprehensive and integrated picture, a way of thinking about the mind that is theoretically coherent and clinically illuminating. He offers a conceptual vocabulary that broadens our understanding, both of the infinitely complex networks of mental life and of the extraordinary potential of psychoanalysis.

Appendix

This book has focused on the fundamentals of Bollas's theory of the mind. For readers who would like to explore other areas of his writing, the following is a chronological list of selected papers in which he addresses psychopathology, psychoanalytic technique, and issues of culture and society.

I Psychopathology

'The trisexual' (SO)

The trisexual seduces members of both sexes in order to gain the other's desire of his self. He is captivating and people feel privileged to be with him, but then relationships are gradually desexualised. He becomes a body without gender – a virgin presence. His aim is to defeat sexuality and transform it into admiration.

'Loving hate' (SO)

Does hate necessarily imply destructiveness? Loving hate can be used to conserve the object, to act out an unconscious form of love, or to compel the object into a passionate relationship. It may preserve an identity in the face of engulfing parental idealisation, the antidote to being seen as the model child, serving a need to express the primitive parts of the self. Some patients create hate in the analyst as a way of ensuring an intimate rapport, because parental anger was the only deeply engaged emotional experience available to them as children. The primary aim of loving hate is to get close to the object.

'Normotic illness' (SO)

A family whose priority is to be conventional can create in the child an exaggerated drive to be normal. Living is based on activities; contact with the subjective internal world is lost, or never truly formed, and this brings about a desymbolisation of mental content. Life involves doing instead of being. Breakdown or attempted suicide may be the only way to refuse the family's normotic structure.

'Extractive introjection' (SO)

Projective identification involves ridding the self of unwanted elements by putting them into someone else. Extractive introjection is the opposite: one person invades another's mind and steals a part of his psychic life, thus depriving him of an aspect of his own thinking. A child who is constantly attacked for his misdemeanours will lose touch with his own guilt and replace it with anxiety. He can end up with a pervasive sense of injustice because he feels denied the right to elements of his own mental life. He feels empty because his psychic content has been extracted.

'The liar' (SO)

Lying is not necessarily the opposite of truth. Psychopathic lying is an expression of the person's psychic reality; it releases unconscious significance and its associated affects. It may originate as a reparative fantasy, such as the attempt to replace absent parents. If the liar can fool people, this confirms his belief that he can manipulate reality and it creates a sense of safety. He needs the lie to actualise his self experience. The analyst's confusion about what is true and what is a lie constitutes the transference of an entire inner environment.

'The ghostline personality' (FD)

Some people turn away from spontaneous contact with the external world and foster alternative objects that exist within a constructed internal mental space, bounded by a 'ghostline'. When an object representation passes this line it is altered and redefined as a unique inner presence. It lives on internally as a spirit, or ghost, that is within the individual's control. There is a profound refusing of the external environment; the ghostline world acts as a containing presence, representing a retrospective foetalisation of self states.

'The anti-narcissist' (FD)

Positive, realistic narcissism is part of health, but some people cultivate a negative narcissism that forecloses the elaboration of the self. Self-denigration and self-recrimination turn into a pervasive, controlling negativity. If the child experiences idolisation by the mother in place of true rapport, he may seek fights with the father to provide a real relationship. Cultivating his actual talents may cause him to be idolised once again, so he sabotages his abilities. He constructs a negative self in order to oppose the mother's thoughtless devotion.

'Violent innocence' (BC)

Denial is not usually seen in object relational terms. However, it becomes violent innocence when a person incriminates the other as a defence. It simplifies the subject's consciousness and locates disturbing phenomena elsewhere. By asking apparently innocent questions designed to produce disturbance, for example, the violent innocent creates confusion in the other whilst disavowing all knowledge of this. A position of innocence is adopted as a denial of the other's perception.

'Preoccupation unto death' (CU)

There is a spectrum that covers passionate concentration, preoccupation and obsession. Obsession stalls the natural work of unconscious life through the creation of false psychic intensities. The obsessive object is a container for evacuated psychic life, and this prevents normal unconscious object use. The patient feels impinged on, driven crazy by the object. Preoccupation does not foreclose inner freedom in the same way, but a mental space is created in which the object exists to the exclusion of all else. Passionate concentration involves a creative, generative channelling of interest in the object for its own sake that assists unconscious exploration of the world.

'Mind against self' (MT)

Psychosis is discussed in terms, not of mental content, but of the structure of the relationship between self and mind. When a person comes to regard his mind with alarm, this is the root of much mental illness. Psychoanalysis is effective with psychosis because the analyst is not alarmed by the patient's mind and can break its power by engaging with its contents. If these patients are instead treated supportively, the toxic cathexes are not challenged and the unconscious meanings not discovered. The implication is that the clinician, too, regards the patient's mind as dangerous and this sustains the core pathology.

'Mental interference' (MT)

In a patient with an entrenched depression, the mind becomes an unempathic, demanding other that continually attacks the self. Rumination replaces thinking, and regression represents an unconscious return to the maternal care of infancy. This weakens the ego, and states of confusion attack generative mental functioning. By providing containment and by analysing the hatred of mental processes, the analyst gradually enlivens the patient, counteracting passive resistance and defensive mental stasis by creating curiosity.

'Dead mother, dead child' (MT)

In the context of a schizoid patient with violent paranoid fantasies, a dichotomy is introduced between the concepts of introject and interject. Whereas an introject stems from the needs or desires of the self, an interject is an internal object resulting from, for example, parental projective identification or a trauma in the real that violates the self. This forceful interruption of the self's idiom produces the sense of a lack of unconsciously generated meaning. The intrusion of the real into the personal causes a suspended state, and the pain caused by the original trauma becomes the primary sense of self. Thoughts feel unsafe because they threaten to become overwhelming events in the real.

'Borderline desire' (MT)

For people who inhabit borderline states, emotional turbulence becomes the primary object of desire. Flying into rages and acting out grievances achieves a recurring effect in the self and this brings satisfaction. Ordinary feelings are escalated into intense, disturbing experiences. In order to establish intimacy, they must force this primary state into the other. They are psychically accident-prone; anything less than catastrophe seems lifeless. Turmoil is chosen in preference to a void.

Hysteria (London: Routledge, 2000)

In this book, Bollas argues that the concept of hysteria has disappeared from contemporary culture, subsumed under other diagnostic categories that obscure the centrality of sexuality. He argues that awareness of sexuality is inherently traumatic as it destroys the primary relation to the mother as caregiver, transforming her into the sexual object of the father and also of the child. The hysterical personality becomes organised around a refusal of knowledge of the body and of sexuality. The chapters deal with different aspects such as sexual epiphany, the functions of the father, seduction, showing off, self as theatre, and the malignant hysteric. Chapters 1 and 14 contain valuable summaries and comparisons of different character disorders.

When the Sun Bursts: the Enigma of Schizophrenia *(Yale, 2015)*

This is an evocative and highly personal account of Bollas's experiences of working with both children and adults who suffer from schizophrenic illness. He explores the structure and the logic of schizophrenic thinking, and makes an impassioned plea for an intensive psychoanalytic approach, emphasising the need for intervention as soon as possible after the illness has set in. He regards it as a tragedy that many schizophrenic patients are treated instead with dehumanising incarceration, mind-altering medications and isolation. Human beings have an inherent instinct to turn to others when in distress, and he argues that even in the most profound states of psychic disturbance this should be the foundation for cure.

II   Psychoanalytic technique

'Self-analysis and the countertransference' (SO)

In psychoanalysis, experiencing must come before interpretation. The capacity for receptivity requires tranquillity – a state of mind that is relaxed rather than vigilant. If the analyst refrains from interpretation this promotes the development of the patient's private world. There are many forms of transference. As the analysis progresses, there is a move away from projective transference to the analyst as an external object, towards transference to the analyst as an internal object, employed as an auxiliary in the process of knowing the self. The classical view of the countertransference was that it should be resolved and evenly hovering attention restored. Latterly it is recognised as an ever-present state of being in the analyst, available to be used by the patient.

'Ordinary regression to dependence' (SO)

During an analysis there will be periods of ordinary, benign regression, in which the analyst suspends active intervention. This allows for a crucial generative process, part of the patient's inner relation to self experiences. As the regression deepens, shifts in the patient's self state will bring different qualities of silence. As he falls into intense, private self-preoccupation, akin to the sensory and the poetic, he becomes immersed in unconscious experiencing.

'Off the wall' (FD)

This paper deals with the analyst's relationship to his own subjectivity: stray thoughts, fantasies, feelings, things he thinks of saying but withholds, gradual changes in his imaginative conception of the patient. Each patient is experienced differently, and much of the analytic work takes place within the analyst. There is a danger in organising the patient into a set of interpretations. The capacity not to know is an accomplishment, and the function of not knowing needs to play an explicit part in interpretations, conveying an element of the analytic sensibility. This aspect of technique, described in terms of the dialectics of difference, mitigates the danger of interpretation interfering with free association.

'The psychoanalyst's celebration of the analysand' (FD)

The psychoanalytic literature is heavily weighted towards consideration of what goes wrong in the human psyche. However, analytic treatment should not consist solely of the negative. It may feel more problematic for the analyst to analyse the patient's life instincts, including love of the analyst. Just as analysis of destructiveness should not be condemnatory, analysis of life instincts should not be either gratifying or approving. There should be recognition and acknowledgement of the pleasure involved in working together, and of the real capacities of the patient, otherwise the analyst risks interfering with experiences of true creative spontaneity.

'The psychoanalyst's multiple function' (FD)

Interpretation alone does not constitute insight. It is only when the patient can use the analyst's offering as an object that he can realise something within himself. Technique must vary according to what is happening. If, for example, positive feelings are invariably interpreted as projections, the patient will feel that his ability to perceive worth in the other is diminished. The various schools of psychoanalysis prioritise different features of mental life, and each therefore provides the patient with a different analytic object. Hence the need for pluralism. The analyst should be an object that performs multiple functions. The patient will unconsciously evoke different parts of the analyst's personality to perform specific functions. We need a 'subject relations theory' that recognises the unique idiom of each person.

'The psychoanalyst's use of free association' (BC)

The analyst uses both his own disseminating subjectivity and an objectifying perspective. Transference and countertransference form an object-relational dialogue that involves a dialectic between simple and complex selves that takes place within both participants. Both will free associate; both will be receptive. The patient's narrative disseminates in the analyst's mind, its logic grasped less through secondary process thinking and more through effects that are close to those of poetry or music. Interpretations are formed out of many elements such as associations, observations, thoughts and images. Psychoanalysis tends to fear the apparently irrational. Is this actually a fear of subjectivity itself? The work of analysis will always be far more complex than any theory.

'A separate sense' (CU)

The analyst develops a separate sense for each patient, derived from the patient's individual aesthetic in being. This involves a unique set of ideas, feelings, visual images and sonic metaphors that implicitly recognise the dense, moving complexity of that patient's elaboration of idiom. Unconsciously, analyst and patient develop a sense of the other as process, choosing which disseminations to follow, designating areas to be investigated, and enabling the formation of psychic gravities that lead to fresh perspectives. These are ordinary forms of the uncanny, part of relational knowing. There is pleasure and gratification, both for the analyst who encounters the patient's idiom and for the patient who experiences this deep recognition.

'On transference interpretation as a resistance to free association' (FM)

This paper is a radical critique of analytic technique that is based on continual interpretation of the transference. The fundamentally unconscious nature of the analytic situation is denied by the analyst who has an agenda. He also sidelines the rest of the patient's mind. Alongside obvious manifestations of the transference, many other lines of unconscious thought will be developing within and around the immediate relational situation. When presenting cases to colleagues, analysts can feel intense pressure to focus on the transference, thus repeating the experience of the patient who is repeatedly confronted with it in the session. Both are liable to comply with the prevailing assumption and provide what the group, or the analyst, expects to hear. A selected fact is therefore transformed into a total truth. This narrow focus constitutes a resistance to engaging with the breadth of unconscious ideas revealed through the process of free association and free listening.

'Free association' (EOW)

Written for the general reader, this is a succinct but comprehensive survey of the topic of free association. It also provides a synthesis of many aspects of Bollas's thinking. He advocates a return to Freud's technique based on free association and evenly suspended attention, emphasising the importance of listening openly to what the patient brings without prejudging its meaning or imposing any hierarchy of significance. The aim is to develop unconscious capabilities in both participants, a process that is therapeutic in itself. He discusses unconscious communication and the deep complexity of associative material in which various forms of logic are present – the logic of sequence, of projection, of transference and countertransference, and of character – and he introduces the idea of a process of question and answer that is inherent in the mind. He regards free association as a form of unconscious thinking that serves the self's drive to elaborate its idiom.

The Infinite Question *(London: Routledge, 2009)*

This book develops further the issues discussed in 'Free association'. It has a more technical focus, using highly detailed commentaries on verbatim case material to demonstrate the unfolding of the sequential logic inherent in the patient's narrative. It also explores many other aspects of free association from both a clinical and a theoretical point of view.

Catch Them Before They Fall *(London: Routledge, 2013)*

Bollas describes a radical approach to the treatment of non-psychotic patients who are at the point of breaking down. This involves continuing with the psychoanalytic work, but (for a limited period) with greatly increased intensity. This provides the opportunity to be with the core of a self, presented in its most vulnerable and undefended state. Bollas believes that in this situation psychoanalysis is the treatment of choice, and that by consigning the patient to medication or hospitalisation the analyst denies the profoundly transformative potential of the breakdown.

When the Sun Bursts: the Enigma of Schizophrenia *(Yale, 2015)*

See the description in section III of this Appendix.

III   Society and culture

' *"Don't worry your father"* ' *(FD)*

This paper explores the place in the child's psyche of the father himself and of the world of the father that exists outside the reality of home. There may be a dual experience of the father as both powerful and fragile, his return home protected and orchestrated by the mother, who offers him a limited version of what has happened in his absence. The father's temporal routines are set against the timelessness of the young child's life with the mother. Fantasies about father's work life provide a prelude to the child's own subsequent engagement with the reality that exists outside the family.

'The fascist state of mind' (BC)

Fascism can exist in the mind of the individual and of the group. Under the pressure of intense need or anxiety, the self/group loses its democratic functioning and starts to project. The mind ceases to be complex as it loses the polysemous character of the symbolic order and begins to operate tyrannically, eliminating all opposition. Instead of doubt, uncertainty and self-interrogation, it employs the pathological function of certainty, and this leaves a moral void. A victim is chosen to contain that void, and he must then be exterminated. Thus a state of mind becomes an act of violence and the process of annihilation is idealised. The process of intellectual genocide involves distortion of the opponent's views, decontextualisation, denigration, caricature and character assassination. There can also be intellectual genocide through omission: opponents are eliminated via an absence of reference to their work or culture.

'The structure of evil' (CU)

In this paper Bollas deepens our understanding of why the word 'evil' has such evocative power. Referring to the book of Genesis, he defines evil as a sequence of events in which the evil person starts by approaching an other who is in need. He offers help which is gratefully accepted, thereby trading upon our most ancient object relation: basic trust in a nurturing other. The victim believes in the goodness of the evil one, who then creates an apocalyptic reversal in which the victim realises that he has trusted one who all along has intended harm. The serial killer epitomises this structure as the victim realises that he or she will be murdered as a result of this trust.

'Creativity and psychoanalysis' (MT)

Art reflects the dense overdetermination of psychic life. Bollas discusses the influence of Freud, and especially of the free associative process, on the intense artistic developments of the 20th century. In particular, abstract expressionism represents unconscious influence that can be observed but not readily comprehended. Freud rejected the significance of the aesthetic element in mental life, but just as psychic reality can be transmuted into an artistic work, the dream materialises the day's internal experiences through a similar transformational process. Free association offers another means of self transformation that enhances the self's unconscious capability.

China on the Mind (London: Routledge, 2013)

Bollas compares broad differences in the mentalities of Eastern and Western civilisations, linking these to the maternal and paternal orders. Eastern thinking favours being; Western prioritises doing. Eastern language is implicit and interpretive; Western verbalisation seeks explicit lucidity. Aspects of our differing psychoanalytic traditions reflect these polarities, and he sees the Freudian approach as having the potential to reunite the two forms of psychic functioning.

The Christopher Bollas Reader (London: Routledge, 2011) is a collection of 16 major papers, most published previously in other volumes, that illustrate the breadth of Bollas's thinking.

Two published interviews with Bollas are particularly illuminating. One, with Anthony Molino, is published in Freely Associated: Encounters in

Psychoanalysis (ed. Molino, A., London: Free Association Books,1997); the other, with Vincenzo Bonaminio, forms the first two chapters of *The Freudian Moment* (London: Routledge, 2007).

*The Vitality of Objects: Exploring the Work of Christopher Bolla*s (ed. Scalia, J., London: Continuum, 2002), is a wide-ranging collection of essays on Bollas's work by Joel Beck, Arne Jemstedt, Adam Phillips, Gabriela Mann, James Grotstein, Anthony Molino and Wesley Shumar, Jacqueline Rose, Joanne Feit Diehl, Michael Szollosy, Greg Drasler and Kate Browne.

Generation: Preoccupations and Conflicts in Contemporary Psychoanalysis by Jean White (London: Routledge, 2006) refers to Bollas's ideas within a broad comparative study of contemporary psychoanalysis.

The Independent Mind in British Psychoanalysis by Eric Rayner (London: Free Association Books, 1990) is an encyclopaedic account of the Independent tradition that includes many references to Bollas's work.

Index

'What is this thing called self?'
33, 38
'Creativity and psychoanalysis'
(Bollas) 62, 72

de Kooning, Willem 2
depressive disorders 54, 65, 71
destiny 25–6
'The destiny drive' (Bollas) 19, 24
'Dissemination' (Bollas) 56, 60, 67
dreams: Bollas' integrated theory on
93–4; dream analysis integration of
psychic dualities 7; free association
in 63, 66, 68, 69; self relationships
in 36–7; unconscious complexity
of 59; unconscious role in
dreamworks 12, 13, 14

ego 11, 14, 16, 21, 23, 24, 26, 28, 35,
38, 55, 63, 71, 76, 79, 90
The Ego and the Id (Freud) 11
European Study Group for
Unconscious Thought 2
'The evocative object' (Bollas) 22,
46, 49, 55
evocative objects: aesthetic dejection
from mismatch with 54; aleatory
objects as 50, 53; 'Architecture
and the unconscious' on 52; art
forms of 52–3; 'Aspects of self
experiencing' on 51; Bollas'
integrated theory on 94; *China on
the Mind* on 52; concentration on
54; 'The evocative object' on 49,
55; *The Evocative Object World* on
46; free association and selection of
66; *The Freudian Moment* on 48–9;
idiom expressed via 47–8, 49–53,
54; inanimate environment of 47,
48; intrinsic value of 47, 48–9, 51;
key concepts in 46; key papers on
46; in metapsychology of Bollas
46–55, 66, 94; mnemic objects
as 49, 50, 53; normotic illness
and selection of 53; obsession
with 54; pathology reflected via
53–4; perceptive identification of
48–9; 'Preoccupation unto death'
on 54; preoccupation with 54;

projective identification of 48–50;
receptive unconscious response
to 47; terminal objects not 50–1,
54; traumatic matrices and 51, 53;
unconscious thinking via selection
of 51–3, 54
The Evocative Object World (Bollas):
'Architecture and the unconscious'
52; 'The evocative object world'
46; 'Free association' 62

Fairbairn, Ronald 46
fate 25–6
fathers *see* paternal order
*Forces of Destiny: Psychoanalysis
and Human Idiom* (Bollas): 'The
anti-narcissist' 37; 'The destiny
drive' 19, 24; 'The ghostline
personality' 37; 'Historical sets and
the conservative process' 83, 91;
'Off the wall' 74, 76, 78; 'A theory
for the true self' 19
free association: analyst's use
of 80–1; 'Creativity and
psychoanalysis' on 72; definition
and description of 64–5;
'Dissemination' on 67; evocative
object selection and 66; 'Free
association' on 62; Freudian Pair
based on 74–82; idiom expressed
via 66; *The Infinite Question* on 62,
68, 69, 70; key concepts in 62; key
papers and books on 62; language
transformers or clichéd phrases in
67; logic of unconscious sequence
in 67–9; in metapsychology
of Bollas 58, 62–72, 74–82,
85–92; music analogy for 68, 69;
'Normotic illness' on 67; phonemic
significance of words in 67;
polysemous words in 67; psychic
dualities reflected via 65; psychic
genera formation via 71; question
and answer process in 69–70;
radical, in unconscious complexity
58; receptive unconscious and 63;
splitting or creative destruction
via 65–6; theoretical pluralistic
approaches to 85–92; therapeutic

value of process of 70–2 (*see also* Freudian Pair)
'Free association' (Bollas) 62
French psychoanalysis 1–2, 67
Freud, Anna 1
Freud, Sigmund: Bollas influenced by 2; on free association 62–6, 68; Freudian Pair based on techniques of 77–80; integrated theory origins with 93; "metapsychology" coined by 93; on nodal points 59; pleasure principle of 26; on repression 11, 12–13, 14, 16, 83, 94; on self objectification 35; structural theory of 11–12, 13–14; theoretical pluralism including concepts of 85–92; thing-presentations concept of 27; topographical theory of 10–11, 13–14; on unconscious 10–13, 23
The Freudian Moment (Bollas): 'Articulations of the unconscious' 10, 56; on evocative objects 48–9; 'On transference interpretation as a resistance to free association' 83, 85; 'Perceptive identification' 46, 83; 'Psychic transformations' 10, 56, 59–60, 83; 'Transference interpretation as a resistance to free association' 74; 'What is theory?' 10, 27, 83–4
Freudian Pair: dialectics of difference in 76–7; free association as basis for 74–82; idiom perception and attunement in 75, 77–8; interformality in 75; key concepts in 74; key papers on 74; in metapsychology of Bollas 74–82; 'The necessary destructions of psychoanalysis' on 81; 'Off the wall' on 76, 78; omniscience illusion avoidance in 76; perceptive identification in 77; psychic dualities symbolized in 78–82; psychic genera in 81–2; 'The psychoanalyst's use of free association' on 80; repression awareness in 76; self state oscillation in 80–1; transference in

79–80; unconscious communication in 77–8; unconscious complexity explored by 80, 81

'The ghostline personality' (Bollas) 37
'The goals of psychoanalysis' (Bollas) 62
Green, André 1

Harris, Matte 1
Heimann, Paula 1
Hepworth, Barbara 22
'Historical sets and the conservative process' (Bollas) 83, 91

id 11, 14, 24, 25–6, 35
idiom: aesthetic moment forming 20–1, 22, 47; artists reflecting personal 22; Bollas' integrated theory on 94, 95–6; character and interrelating influenced by 41, 42–4, 45; communication congruency with 59; *Cracking Up* on 23; 'The destiny drive' on 24; 'The evocative object' on 22; evocative objects reflecting 47–8, 49–53, 54; expression and elaboration of 25–6, 47–8, 49–53, 54; fate and destiny in relation to 25–6; form *vs.* content reflecting 22–3; free association expressing 66; Freudian Pair perception and attunement of 75, 77–8; as kernel of self 19–20, 25, 94; key concepts in 19; key papers on 19; maternal 28, 31; maternal role in acknowledging 20–1, 23, 37, 47; receptive unconscious in relation to 21–2, 25; self relationships impacted by 37–8; 'The spirit of the object as the hand of fate' on 20–1; transformational object for 20, 23, 47; 'The transformational object' on 20; traumatic matrices impacting 21–2, 24–5; true self concept *vs.* 23–4; unthought known influenced by 28–9, 30–1
The Infinite Question (Bollas) 56, 57, 62, 68, 69, 70

free association reflecting 65;
Freudian Pair symbolizing 78–82;
of maternal and paternal orders
6–8, 78–80; in metapsychology of
Bollas 6–9, 65, 78–82, 94–5
psychic genera: Bollas' integrated
theory on 94; definition and
description of 15, 34; free
association and formation of
71; Freudian Pair evolving
81–2; intuition links to 17;
'Psychic genera' on 16; receptive
unconscious and 14–17, 21–2; self
composed of 33–4; unconscious
complexity creating 59–60
'Psychic genera' (Bollas) 10, 16
'Psychic transformations' (Bollas) 10,
56, 59–60, 83
psychoanalysis: Bollas'
metapsychology of (see
metapsychology of Bollas); British
1, 2, 4, 46, 63, 84–92; French 1–2,
67; Freudian (see Freud, Sigmund)
'The psychoanalyst's use of free
association' (Bollas) 74, 80
psychopathology: borderline
personality as 70–1; depressive
disorders as 54, 65, 71; normotic
illness as 37–8, 53; obsession as
54, 65; psychotic illness as 38–9;
schizophrenia as 1, 37, 38–9, 71
psychotic illness 38–9

receptive unconscious: *Being a
Character* on 14; Bollas' integrated
theory of 93–6; evocative objects
in 47; free association and 63;
Freud's structural theory on
11–12, 13–14; idiom in terms of
21–2, 25; key concepts in 10; key
papers on 10; in metapsychology
of Bollas 10–17, 21–2, 25, 42–3,
47, 63, 93–6; psychic genera and
14–17, 21–2; 'Psychic genera' on
16; repression *vs.* receptivity in
11, 12–13, 14, 15–17; traumatic
matrices impacting 11, 16,
21–2, 25; unconscious character
reception in 43; unconscious

communication in 13, 14, 42–3,
94–5; unconscious creativity in 12,
14, 94; unconscious perception in
12–13, 14, 94; 'What is theory?'
on 10
regression 88–9
repression: Freudian Pair awareness
of 76; Freud on 11, 12–13, 14, 16,
83, 94; receptivity *vs.* 11, 12–13,
14, 15–17

schizophrenia 1, 37, 38–9, 71
'The self as object' (Bollas) 33, 35
self presentation 43–5, 75
self relationships: 'The anti-narcissist'
on 37; awareness of self in 37–8;
'Being a character' on 39; body in
35; disorder or psychopathology
in 37–9; dreams reflecting 36–7;
'The ghostline personality' on 37;
idiom impacting 37–8; internal
conversations in 34; key concept
in 33; key papers on 33; in
metapsychology of Bollas 33–9;
'Mind against self' on 35–6, 38;
mind in 35–6, 38–9; 'Normotic
illness' on 37–8; plurality of 33,
35, 39; psychic genera in 33–4;
'The self as object' on 35; self
objectification in 34–7, 38–9; 'The
trisexual' on 37; unity of 33, 39;
'What is this thing called self?' on
33, 38; 'The wisdom of the dream'
on 36
self representation 43–5
*The Shadow of the Object:
Psychoanalysis of the Unthought
Known* (Bollas): 'Moods and
the conservative process' 27,
29; 'Normotic illness' 37–8,
67; 'Ordinary regression to
dependence' 83, 88; 'The self as
object' 33, 35; on self relationships
33, 35, 37–8, 39; 'The spirit of
the object as the hand of fate'
20–1, 46; 'The transformational
object' 19, 20; 'The trisexual'
37; 'The unthought known: early
considerations' 27, 31